I0760100

The Plant Book

Lady Chatterley's Lover
D.H. Lawrence
stephen fry the fry chronicles
NIX
BOY SWALLOWS UNIVERSE
TRENT DALTON
TOM KENEALLY The People's Train
RUSSIA
BRYSON ONE SUMMER
the first move

The Plant Book

The ultimate guide to thriving houseplants

Tammy Huynh

murdoch books
Sydney | London

Contents

Part Two
Plant Profiles and Care 51

Contents

Introduction

Welcome to the wonderful world of plants.

When it comes to growing plants, it's easy to assume that the basics are straightforward. We learned in school or by observation that plants need sunlight and water, so how hard can it be? Many of us place our plants in the brightest spot in the house and water them regularly, believing that we're doing everything right. However, without understanding the unique needs of each plant, we may inadvertently set them up for struggle rather than success.

When our plants die, we might think it's a plant problem rather than a learning opportunity. So, we try to grow the same plants in the same way again, only to encounter similar results.

The truth is that we all have green thumbs - we simply need to learn how to nurture them. Just like when we learned to ride a bike or manage a house, some things come easier than others. Caring for plants is no different.

To ensure that our plants thrive indoors, it's crucial to understand their natural growing environment. This knowledge will help us to determine their ideal conditions - how much light, humidity and water they need - making it easier for us to succeed in our growing efforts. Fortunately, most plants can often tolerate some variation in their care.

A bit about me

My passion for plants started with my late 'po po', my maternal grandmother, who came to live with us when I was a child. She fled the Vietnam War and resided in refugee camps before my mum was granted the opportunity to live in Australia and eventually sponsored her mother to join us. My grandma grew plants out of necessity, having gardened in Vietnam to produce food to sell at the markets and feed her family. Over time, gardening became a cherished pastime, where we kids would play and 'help' her in the garden. We were spoilt with fresh, homegrown produce, although we didn't realise at the time how fortunate we were.

At the end of high school, I aspired to a career in psychology, intrigued by how the human mind works and eager to understand it better. It was my dad who planted the seed - pardon the pun - of studying agriculture. 'But you escaped a hard farming life in Vietnam,' I said to him. 'Why would I want to study farming?' My dad had recently purchased some property and was keen on starting a bamboo farm. Surprisingly, I decided to follow this path.

After a year of studying agriculture at The University of Sydney, I switched to horticulture - until then, I didn't even know that the dedicated study of plants existed. I was hooked, leading me to an Honours thesis on bamboo.

From there, I took on roles with the *Better Homes and Gardens* magazine and Yates, and at some point along the way I decided to study landscape design, so I could deepen my understanding of plants and how they're used in design. The years became a blur of projects, experiences and learning opportunities, including helping my parents plant and harvest edible bamboo shoots.

Eventually, I left full-time work and started my own plant-related business, Leaf an Impression, in 2019. I host plant workshops, speak at events, write gardening content for magazines and online platforms, and provide garden consultations - basically, anything plant-related! In 2022, I landed the dream gig of becoming a presenter on Australia's longest-running TV gardening program, *Gardening Australia*. I still pinch myself daily!

My passion for plants and gardening has only grown, driving me to continue to inspire and share the joy of gardening with others ... to *leaf an impression*.

Tammy Huynh

Houseplant Care 101

Part One

In this section, we'll cover the essentials of houseplant care, breaking down everything you need to know to cultivate healthy, thriving indoor plants. From understanding light requirements and choosing the right potting mix to boosting humidity and tackling pests and diseases, these practical tips will help you confidently care for your plants.

Plus, there's a dedicated troubleshooting guide designed to help you identify and resolve issues that may arise with your plants.

Lighting

Lighting is perhaps the most crucial aspect of plant care. Plants rely on light to convert water and carbon dioxide into energy through photosynthesis. Without adequate light, no amount of watering, feeding or love can save your plant; it will struggle to thrive.

While some plants have adapted to low-light conditions, they often employ clever strategies to capture as much light as possible. For instance, many shade-tolerant plants have large leaves to enhance light absorption in dappled sunlight.

How much light?

For the most part, indoor plants need some level of light, from direct sun to low light. If you find some of the terms below confusing, then it may be a good idea to purchase a light meter. It will help you to better understand how much light a room receives. Some books and websites highlight the lux or foot-candle requirements of different plants, making it easy to pinpoint the ideal lighting conditions for your plants.

Direct sun

When the sun's rays shine directly on the plant for most of the day without any obstructions (such as curtains or nearby buildings), this is classified as direct sun. This intense light can scorch most indoor plants, with the exception of cacti and succulents.

Bright, indirect light or filtered light

This is the sweet spot for most indoor plants, and the light requirement for most of the plants listed in this book. It provides plenty of diffused light - often with some direct sun in the morning and remaining bright for most of the day. You can achieve this with sheer curtains, Venetian blinds, skylights or frosted windows, which help to prevent harsh rays from directly hitting the plant. Many of our indoor plants originate from tropical and subtropical rainforests, where they thrive under the dappled light of a canopy, making bright, indirect light ideal for their growth.

Someone once said to me, 'If you can read a book comfortably in that spot for four to six hours without additional light, then this is the perfect place for a plant.' I think that's a great test for bright, indirect light!

Medium light

Plants located further back from the window, perhaps in the centre of the room, typically receive medium light.

Low light

This area receives little sunlight throughout the day. While not many plants can tolerate such conditions, a select few species are adapted to survive in these environments. These plants may persist in low light, but they won't necessarily thrive, often exhibiting slower growth and less vibrant foliage. But note that 'low' light is not the same as 'no' light. There are no plants that will survive in total darkness. You could position them there temporarily, but it's best to give them a position with some light. See 'Low light' on page 47.

When low light equals leggy growth
A plant that looks sparse, with extended internodes - the spaces between two nodes (bumps on stems where new leaves grow) - is often referred to as 'leggy' and is experiencing a phenomenon known as etiolation. When a plant is grown in dim conditions and has to stretch to seek out light, it becomes elongated; this leads to weak and spindly growth. The stems may contort as they bend towards the light, and the leaves may drop.

To fix this, trim the plant back to the area where it appears fullest or bushiest, making sure to cut just above a leaf node. For succulents, this may mean cutting them back to near ground level. Additionally, reposition the plant in a brighter location to encourage healthy growth. Keep in mind that the increased light exposure may mean that the plant requires more frequent watering, so be sure to regularly check the moisture in the potting mix.

Grow lights

If your home doesn't have enough natural light, or you want to optimise plant growth, then grow lights are a great option. Once reserved for commercial growers thanks to their hefty price tag, grow lights are now far more accessible thanks to advancements in technology. Over the last decade, improvements in LED technology have not only increased affordability but also expanded the range of options available, from simple bulbs that fit into regular lamps to sleek, purpose-built fixtures designed for style and functionality.

There are different grades, from entry-level to premium, but in general a standard grow light is sufficient. However, like with anything, if you choose to invest more, you will see better results.

You don't need to worry too much about technical details such as lux, lumens or Kelvins because many lights are marketed specifically as 'grow lights' for plant enthusiasts, making it much easier to choose the right one. Simply look for full-spectrum grow lights, which include the wavelengths that are most important for photosynthesis, to ensure that your plants get the light they need without the hassle of you sifting through complicated specifications.

Watch out for sunburn
As the angle of the sun changes in summer, a plant you had sitting in bright light close to a window may become more exposed to direct sun. On days with extreme heat, the direct sun and/or radiant heat from the window may cause the foliage to burn. Leaves may develop brown or black patches or appear pale and bleached, especially on the side exposed to the light. They may also become crispy or wilt. Remove the affected growth, and move the plant out of direct sun to prevent further damage.

Potting mix and other growing mediums

Most plants need a substrate for growth. You can find various bagged potting mixes at your local nursery or garden centre, so which one is right for your plants? Once you understand what your plants need and the ingredients that go into making different potting mixes, it's much easier to choose the correct one. You can also make your own potting mix, which is sometimes necessary depending on the type of plants you're growing.

In Australia, the quality of potting mixes is indicated by five ticks on the Australian Standard logo, which ensures consistent quality in terms of aeration, water-holding capacity and pH balance. There are two grades of potting mix you can purchase at garden centres: regular and premium. The regular mix, marked with a black logo, lacks added components (such as fertilisers or wetting agents), meaning that you have to incorporate these at planting. In contrast, the premium mix, identified by a red logo, usually contains nutrients that can sustain your plants for three to six months. The price difference between the two is often just a few dollars, making it worthwhile to invest in the premium option when possible.

A general-purpose premium potting mix is suitable for most plants and often features a high proportion of composted organic materials (such as pine bark or sawdust). This potting mix is lightweight and easy to handle, but it can compact over time, reducing vital air pockets and depriving roots of oxygen. To maintain the structural integrity of the potting mix, consider adding perlite – a versatile, lightweight mineral that remains stable and doesn't break down.

However, specific plants – such as cacti, succulents, orchids, African violets and certain aroids – require either specialty mixes (which can be found in garden centres and nurseries) or tailored homemade blends. For example, a cacti and succulent mix contains higher proportions of sand and grit to reflect the arid environment in which these plants thrive, ensuring excellent drainage. Orchids are primarily epiphytes (plants that grow on other plants) and grow in the wild on trees, anchoring themselves to bark or other surfaces rather than in soil; thus, an orchid-specific mix – often composed of various sizes of pine bark – mimics these natural conditions.

While pre-bagged mixes are convenient, they can become costly, especially if you're expanding your plant collection. In such cases, investing in a few key ingredients to create your own mixes might be the best approach.

Around the world

In regions such as Aotearoa New Zealand, the United Kingdom and North America (including the United States, Canada and Mexico), bagged potting mixes are produced according to local standards. However, there are no standardised labels or symbols to clearly identify premium versus basic products. Potting mixes may have branding, their own labelling or endorsements from associations to help differentiate them.

Potting mix ingredients

Understanding the role that each ingredient plays in potting mix will help you to appreciate its purpose. You may come across recipes with varying ratios and percentages, but as you become familiar with the ingredients, you may like to experiment with your own blends.

Horticultural charcoal
A porous, carbon-rich material, it's created through the pyrolysis (oxygen-free heating) of organic materials, such as wood or coconut husks. When added to potting mixes, it improves drainage, absorbs excess moisture and impurities, and provides a habitat for beneficial microbes.

Homemade compost
This nutrient-rich organic material is made from decomposed plant and animal matter. High in organic elements, it supports beneficial microorganisms in the growing medium and retains moisture effectively.

Perlite
This is a lightweight volcanic mineral that has been heated to expand, creating a porous structure. It helps to aerate potting mixes, prevents compaction, improves drainage and retains moisture. Perlite can also be used as a stand-alone growing medium. Always rinse it before use so the fine dust particles don't settle in your potting mix or cause any respiratory irritations.

Washed river sand
This coarse material improves drainage and aeration in potting mixes. Its large particles prevent compaction, making it ideal for plants that thrive in well-drained conditions.

Orchid bark
This comprises bark chips in various sizes or grades. Its chunky texture promotes air circulation and moisture retention, making it suitable as a stand-alone growing medium – especially for orchids – or as an additive to improve drainage and retain moisture.

Premium potting mix
A lightweight blend rich in organic materials, this quality potting mix is designed to provide adequate drainage and aeration for pot plants. It typically contains a mix of composted sawdust or pine bark and other additives, ensuring optimal moisture retention and nutrient availability.

Coco peat or coir peat
Made from the husk of coconuts, it's high in organic matter and a valuable addition to potting mix. It improves structure, retains moisture and helps keep the mix light and airy. It also serves as an environmentally friendly alternative to peat moss.

Safety note
When handling potting mix or additives, always work in a well-ventilated area. Potting mix may contain *Legionella* bacteria, which can cause Legionnaires' disease if inhaled. Good ventilation helps to reduce the risk of exposure. Also consider wearing gloves to protect your hands from potential irritants.

HELVETIA

Watering

Have you ever been given prescriptive advice on watering your plants? It sounds helpful to know that you need to 'water once weekly' or 'water every fortnight with half a cup of water', but this may not be the best advice. In fact, it could be detrimental to your plants' health.

Your home's conditions can vary from those found in other houses - for example, you might keep windows open more often or have the heater or air conditioner running constantly. These factors can dry out your plants faster, meaning that you may need to water them more often than the prescribed schedule. Plus, the general advice doesn't account for seasonal changes. As temperatures drop in autumn and winter, your plants will need less water because of slower growth and reduced evaporation.

When and how to water

What's the best way to work out when to water? Rely on your trusty index finger. Simply insert it into the top of the potting mix, down to about the second knuckle, or 2.5-5 centimetres (1-2 inches). If the potting mix feels dry at that depth, then it's time to water. If it still feels moist, then wait a few more days and check again. This method helps to prevent overwatering and ensures that your plants get the right amount of moisture.

You can use a moisture meter to determine if the potting mix is moist or dry. However, I've found that they aren't always reliable. Issues such as poor calibration, inconsistent readings or hitting a dry pocket in the potting mix can give the impression that the entire pot is dry, leading to unnecessary watering. I'd recommend the finger test or gauging the moisture by lifting the pot - a dry pot will feel noticeably lighter.

When watering, ensure that the water runs through the drainage holes at the bottom of the pot. This will confirm that the entire root ball is adequately saturated, and your plant has had a sufficient drink. However, this can sometimes be misleading. Over time, potting mix can become compacted and hydrophobic (water repellent), causing water to run down the inside of the pot instead of soaking into the potting mix. As a result, it may appear that the plant is being properly watered when, in fact, the roots are not receiving enough moisture.

If you notice that your plant is constantly wilted or that the leaves are yellowing and drying despite your best watering efforts, then this may be a sign that your potting mix is hydrophobic. Refer to page 41 of the Troubleshooting section to confirm if this is the issue. If it is, then the potting mix can be treated with a wetting agent, or the pot plant should be completely submerged in a bucket of water or repotted into fresh mix (see 'Repotting plants' on pages 36-7).

Curling leaves
Leaves that are rolled up or curled tightly are often signs of moisture stress. Extreme temperatures can cause leaves to curl as a protective mechanism to prevent rapid water loss. Similarly, underwatering can cause leaves to curl to minimise water loss. Give the plant a good drink, ensuring that the water runs through the drainage holes at the bottom of the pot.

If leaf curling continues to happen, then other factors may be affecting how quickly the potting mix dries out. Large changes in temperature and light intensity can increase the plant's water consumption, requiring you to either water more frequently - always check the potting mix moisture before watering - or relocate the plant to a different area. Additionally, compacted potting mix (see 'Potting mix compaction' on page 49) may prevent adequate water absorption, and root-bound plants will require repotting into fresh potting mix (see 'Repotting plants' on pages 36-7).

Bottom watering

You may have come across terms such as 'bottom watering' or 'butt chugging'. Both describe a method of watering plants where the water is applied to the bottom of the pot, rather than the top of the potting mix. The process involves placing a pot plant in a shallow bucket filled with water, allowing the water level to reach about one-third to halfway up the pot, and leaving it for 20-30 minutes. The theory is that the dry potting mix absorbs the water through the drainage holes; the water is then taken up by the plant roots, effectively watering the plant.

However, this can lead to a build-up of minerals in the potting mix and also raise the pH, which makes certain nutrients unavailable to the plant. These factors can negatively affect plant health. Therefore, it's best to water from the top. This ensures that minerals in the water are moving down through the potting mix; if they're not taken up by the plant, then they're washed out through the drainage holes.

Bottom watering does have its place if your potting mix has become hydrophobic (water repellent) because it has been left too long without watering. However, I prefer to submerge the whole pot, up to the level of the potting mix, in a bucket of water to remedy this. If you don't have the space to do this, then you can fill a saucer or shallow tub with water, place the plant (pot and all) in it, and continue to top up the water once it has been absorbed, until the surface of the potting mix becomes wet. Once it's wet, remove the plant from the saucer or tub and start watering as normal from the top to help flush out any minerals that may have accumulated in the potting mix due to bottom watering.

Water quality
You may have heard claims that watering with tap or town water is bad for your plants. It really depends on your location. However, most town-water supplies need to meet certain guidelines, so it's unlikely that your water source would be contaminated with heavy metals or minerals that could affect plant growth. Personally, I've watered mine without any issues. If you're concerned about chlorine, then there are three ways to reduce the level in the water before you use it on your plants:

1. Pour the water into a jug, and let it sit at room temperature for at least 24 hours.
2. Boil the water continuously for 15 minutes, and then allow it to cool.
3. Purchase and use a dechlorinator.

Rainwater is another great option - I like to bring my plants outside when it's raining or collect rainwater in buckets for indoor watering.

Fertiliser

You only have to walk into the fertiliser aisle of your nursery or garden centre to be instantly confused about what product you need for your plants. With myriad options – such as controlled-release, liquid, granular, slow-release and specialty fertilisers – trying to choose the right one can be overwhelming. Each type of fertiliser serves a specific purpose and caters for a particular plant need, making it essential to understand the different fertiliser types so you can provide optimal care for your greenery.

But why do you need to feed plants? Don't they get their 'food' or energy from the sun? Yes, they do, but sunlight is just one part of the equation. Plants harness sunlight through photosynthesis, converting light energy into chemical energy. However, they also require essential nutrients – such as nitrogen, phosphorus, potassium and trace minerals (for example, calcium, magnesium, iron and sulphur) – from the soil or potting mix to support growth, flowering and overall health. Without these nutrients, even the most well-lit plants can struggle to thrive.

Initially, indoor plants may thrive by using the nutrients available in the potting mix. Over time, however, the mix will become depleted of essential nutrients due to leaching and plant uptake.

So, how do you choose the best fertiliser for your plant? Start by examining the product label for a nutrient table or breakdown. The key nutrients to focus on are nitrogen, phosphorus and potassium – collectively known as macronutrients – since these are consumed in larger quantities by plants.

Nitrogen (N)
Essential for plant development, it promotes lush, leafy green growth. It's ideal for feeding foliage plants.

Phosphorus (P)
It stimulates root growth and helps to promote flowering.

Potassium (K)
This supports flowering and strengthens cell walls, enhancing a plant's resilience to adverse conditions.

The percentage of each macronutrient in the fertiliser (known as the NPK ratio) will differ between products, so choose a fertiliser based on what you're trying to achieve. For instance, if you're nurturing foliage plants, then a fertiliser that is high in nitrogen is beneficial, while flowering plants will thrive with a fertiliser that has increased potassium. In addition to NPK, plants also require small amounts of other nutrients (such as calcium, magnesium and sulphur), although these are needed in lesser quantities.

As the popularity of indoor plants has boomed in the last decade, you'll often see products marketed specifically as indoor-plant fertilisers. They generally have equal amounts of nitrogen and potassium, with a low phosphorus content. This formulation is designed to support lush foliage growth and overall plant health. I recommend examining the nutrient tables to compare products and to avoid overspending based on marketing alone.

Types of fertiliser

Now that you have a grasp on the fundamentals of plant nutrition, let's explore the different types of fertilisers, focusing specifically on those typically used for indoor plants.

It's important to note that both soluble and liquid forms of fertiliser act quickly, providing an immediate nutrient boost, but they need to be applied more frequently than slow- or controlled-release products. All options effectively nourish your plants, so the best choice depends on your personal preference. For instance, if you're often away or find feeding your plants a chore, then slow- or controlled-release fertilisers may better suit your lifestyle. Conversely, if you want to give your plants a boost during the growing season, soluble or liquid fertilisers will deliver rapid results. Don't forget to consider price as an important factor, too.

Soluble
It comes in powder or fine granular form, which you can easily dissolve in water. Use a watering-can to apply the fertiliser.

Liquid
It comes in a ready-made, easy-to-pour format. This allows for straightforward application directly to the plant in a similar way to soluble fertiliser.

Organic, slow release
Available in granules or pellets that break down in the potting mix over time, this fertiliser gradually releases nutrients to the plant while also enriching the mix. It enhances microbial activity, promotes a healthier growing environment and improves moisture retention. However, the rate and duration of breakdown are not precisely controlled, typically lasting two to three months. It's generally lower in NPK because the source of nutrients is organic, unlike synthetic formulations that provide higher levels of plant nutrients but do little to improve the structure of the potting mix.

Controlled release
It contains a balanced dose of nutrients encapsulated in polymer-coated pellets or prills, releasing the nutrients as the plant requires them or as environmental conditions change - typically in response to temperature. Nutrients are often released when the potting mix warms up, indicating active plant growth.

A note on seaweed
Despite popular marketing, seaweed is not a fertiliser - it doesn't supply essential nutrients to plants. Instead, it promotes strong root development and enhances a plant's ability to cope with and recover from environmental stresses, such as drought, frost, and pest or disease attacks. It's also beneficial to use diluted seaweed extract after repotting to help alleviate transplant shock.

When to fertilise your plants

Feeding your plants is most effective when they're actively growing, usually during the warmer months. However, if your plants are in a climate-controlled environment, then they might continue growing through the cooler seasons; feeding them during this time can support their growth.

The frequency of fertiliser application depends on the type of fertiliser you choose. Liquid fertilisers act fast because the nutrients are readily available for roots to absorb. However, they also tend to leach out of the potting mix, which is why they typically need to be applied weekly or fortnightly. Always follow the manufacturer's instructions for application rates and frequency to avoid overfeeding, which can harm the plant (see 'Excess nutrients' on page 46).

Humidity

Many of the species we grow as houseplants come from subtropical and tropical rainforests, where they thrive in warm, moist and humid environments. While these plants are adaptable to indoor living, some are fussier and require higher humidity levels to flourish. Factors such as open windows and doors, cold draughts and climate-control devices can drastically reduce indoor humidity, causing leaves to lose moisture faster than the roots can replace it, often resulting in brown leaf edges. Think about how your skin feels when exposed to air conditioning or heaters - pretty dry, right?

In the cooler months, humidity in the home tends to drop because of heating, but also because cold air holds less moisture than warm air. While plants may not be actively growing during winter, it's still important to maintain proper humidity to prevent plant stress and foliage damage. Similarly, during the warmer months, while the air may be naturally more humid, open windows or air conditioning can still dry out the indoor environment.

To ensure that your plants remain healthy, it's important to monitor and adjust indoor humidity levels throughout the year. You can measure humidity with a hygrometer, which is available in both digital and analogue versions. This device typically displays both temperature and relative humidity, making it useful for checking indoor conditions. You can find hygrometers fairly cheaply online, and they're great for helping you to maintain the right environment for your plants.

To mist or not to mist

Misting can provide a temporary boost in humidity, but it's usually too short-lived to have a significant impact on most plants. The moisture from misting evaporates quickly, especially in dry indoor environments, so it's not an effective long-term solution for plants that require consistently higher humidity.

If you enjoy misting your plants as part of your routine - I know many who do - it can still be helpful for cleaning leaves and providing a little refreshment. However, to maintain proper humidity levels it's better to group plants together or to use a pebble tray or humidifier.

Ways to boost humidity

If you find that the humidity in your home has dropped below what's comfortable for your plants, then there are a few ways you can increase it.

Group plants together
As plants release moisture through transpiration, the air around them naturally becomes more humid. The more plants you have, the stronger this microclimate effect becomes – so feel free to cluster a few plants together. Avoid putting cacti and succulents together with humidity-loving plants, though, as cacti and succulents thrive in dry conditions and prefer low humidity.

Use a pebble tray with water
Fill a shallow tray with pebbles, then add water until it's just below the top of the stones. Place your plant on top, ensuring that the base isn't sitting directly in the water. As the water evaporates, it creates a more humid environment around your plant. Just be sure to keep the water topped up!

Add water bowls
Place small bowls of water around your plants. As the water evaporates, it sends moisture into the air and creates a humid microclimate around nearby plants. Using bowls that are shallow and wide increases the surface area for evaporation, which enhances the effect. While not the most decorative option, it is easy, convenient and low maintenance.

Employ a humidifier
This is a great solution for maintaining consistent humidity levels in your home, especially within an enclosed space. It works by releasing water vapour into the air, which can help to counteract the drying effects of air conditioning and heating. With the rise of indoor plants, you can now find small, USB-powered units that are perfect for shelves or mini greenhouses. Just be sure to monitor the humidity levels, as too much moisture can lead to other issues (such as mould and mildew).

Position in the bathroom
It can be a great spot for humidity-loving plants since it tends to stay more humid than the rest of the home, especially after showers or baths. Even though the humidity might dissipate quickly when the extractor fan is turned on or the door is opened, the bathroom still provides regular moisture boosts that can benefit plants such as calatheas (*Goeppertia* spp.), ferns and orchids. This set-up is especially useful if your bathroom also receives plenty of bright, indirect light.

Install a mini greenhouse
Essentially, this is a small, enclosed space that traps moisture and heat, making it ideal for plants that need extra humidity (such as ferns and tropical species). You can buy mini greenhouses or make your own using a clear plastic container or a glass cloche. Occasionally, open or lift the cover to allow for airflow. If your plants are too big for a mini greenhouse, then try converting a glass cabinet into a small greenhouse (you'll find a plethora of tutorials about this online). It looks quite stylish and is great for maintaining a tropical environment for your plants.

Aesop

Pests and diseases

Despite being indoors and in a somewhat protected environment, houseplants are not immune to pests and diseases. Pests can be blown in through open windows, hide on newly purchased plants, lurk in potting mix or even hitch a ride on your pet's fur. As these pests feed on your plants, they can spread diseases that they have picked up from other plants. Additionally, diseases can spread through spores floating in the air or clinging to your clothing. They may already be present on a plant when you buy it, even if they're not immediately visible. Overwatering, poor airflow and high humidity create an environment in which these dormant spores can thrive and spread.

Healthy plants are less susceptible to attack. Think of your own immune system: when you're feeling good and on top of your game, you're less vulnerable to pathogens. However, when you're run-down, stressed and not caring for yourself properly, a cold can hit you harder and it takes you longer to recover. The same principle applies to plants. Healthy plants - nurtured with the right light, water and nutrients - develop a robust immune system that makes them less vulnerable to pests and diseases. Conversely, stressed or neglected plants become more prone to problems. Just as you would prioritise self-care to boost your immune system, providing consistent and attentive care to your plants strengthens their resilience.

As a plant parent, there's no need to be alarmed - just be aware that pests and diseases are part and parcel of keeping plants. Knowing how to recognise the signs and symptoms of infestations or illnesses is crucial, as is understanding how to treat these issues and prevent them from recurring in the future. Pests aren't always easy to spot; they may be hiding in leaf sheaths or be so tiny that they go unnoticed. As a result, you might see the damage they cause before you ever locate the pests themselves.

Fungus gnats
small, black, flying insects

Identifying features
Resembling fruit flies, these insects measure about 3 millimetres (1/8 inch) in length and have slender bodies with delicate wings. You may notice them hovering around the top of the potting mix, near a light source or - because of their erratic flight patterns or attraction to the carbon dioxide we exhale - close to your face!

Signs of damage
While adult fungus gnats don't harm houseplants, their presence can be quite annoying as they flit around. Similarly, their larvae, which inhabit the potting mix and feed on organic matter, are generally harmless to established plants. However, they do contribute to the ongoing life cycle of these pests.

Control
Fungus gnats thrive in moist environments, especially in potting mix that hasn't dried out because of overwatering or poor drainage. To reduce the risk of infestation, allow the potting mix to dry out between waterings, and ensure that pots have clear drainage holes.

Treat infested plants with neem oil or another suitable insecticide. Consider using sticky traps to catch adult gnats, but ensure that you dispose of these carefully in the bin to avoid harming beneficial insects or wildlife.

Adding a layer of fine pumice on top of the potting mix can prevent adult gnats from laying eggs. This effectively disrupts their breeding cycle without harming other wildlife.

Mealybugs
white, cottony fluff

Identifying features
Small, soft-bodied insects are covered in a white, waxy, cotton-like substance. They tend to cluster in sheltered areas of plants, such as where leaves join the stems, along leaf veins or on new growth. Their white, cottony appearance makes them relatively easy to see, especially when the infestation becomes more severe.

Signs of damage
Mealybugs are sap-sucking insects: they feed on the plant's sap, weakening the plant over time. You may notice yellowing leaves, stunted growth or even leaf drop. Mealybugs also excrete a substance known as honeydew, which makes leaves and other affected plant parts sticky.

Control
Spray the plant with an insecticidal soap or horticultural oil, ensuring that you cover all of the affected areas, including the underside of leaves. For severe infestations, prune off the worst-affected growth to remove clusters of mealybugs, and then spray the plant thoroughly. Repeat treatments may be necessary.

Be careful
Some plants (such as ferns and palms) are sensitive to horticultural oil. It's best to test it on a small, inconspicuous area of the plant first. Wait for a few days to see if there are any adverse reactions (such as burnt or shrivelled foliage) before applying the treatment widely.

Scale
small, soft or hard bumps or shells

Identifying features
Small, round or oval bumps are found on plant stems or leaves. They can be soft or hard, depending on the type of scale. Unlike other pests, they don't move around much once they latch on to a plant and develop their protective shell, which can be brown, black, grey, soft pink or translucent. You can scratch them off with your fingernail.

Signs of damage
Scale insects feed by sucking sap from the plant, causing yellowing, stunted growth or leaf drop over time. A sticky substance called honeydew is often left behind.

Control
For small infestations, gently scrape off the scale insects with a soft cloth, fingernail or old toothbrush. If a spray is necessary, then use an oil-based product because this smothers the protective coating, effectively suffocating the pests. Alternatively, look for a systemic insecticide that is absorbed by the plant and ingested by the pests when they feed.

Thrips
coloured specks crawling on leaves

Identifying features
These tiny, slender insects typically measure around 1–2 millimetres (less than $^1/_{16}$ inch) in length. Adults can be yellow, brown or black with wings that enable them to fly. The larvae are usually pale yellow or green and wingless. Dark brown-black droppings may be seen on the leaves.

Signs of damage
Thrips feed on plant sap, leading to silvery or mottled patches on leaves.

Control
Treat affected plants with an insecticidal soap or horticultural oil, ensuring that you thoroughly cover both the upper and lower surfaces of the leaves. (See the 'Be careful' section above for important information about the use of horticultural oil.)

Spider mites

microscopic pests with webbing

Identifying features
Barely visible pests, they are best recognised by the fine, silk-like webbing they create on affected plants.

Signs of damage
Silvery mottling or yellowing of leaves can indicate damage caused by their feeding. These pests thrive in warm, dry environments, making plants living in such conditions more susceptible to infestations.

Control
Treat plants with an insecticidal soap or horticultural oil, ensuring that you thoroughly cover both the upper and lower surfaces of the leaves. Spray well because these products are contact sprays so pests need to be covered for effective control. (See the 'Be careful' section on page 29 for important information about the use of horticultural oil.) Alternatively, look for a miticide that is absorbed by the plant and ingested by the pests when they feed, such as products containing abamectin.

Aphids

small, soft-bodied insects with long antennae

Identifying features
Small, soft-bodied, pear-shaped insects, they are less than 3 millimetres (1/8 inch) in length and can be green, yellow, orange, pink, brown or black. They're generally found in clusters on the back of leaves, along stems or crowded on new growth.

Signs of damage
Their presence is often signalled by yellowing leaves or distorted growth. They also secrete a sticky honeydew substance as they feed.

Control
Treat plants with an insecticidal soap or horticultural oil. Spray well because these products are contact sprays so pests need to be covered for effective control. (See the 'Be careful' section on page 29 for important information about the use of horticultural oil.) Alternatively, look for a systemic insecticide that is absorbed by the plant and ingested by the pests when they feed.

Sticky leaves
Have you noticed a shiny residue on leaves? Or perhaps felt something sticky when handling your plants? This is likely due to the presence of sap-sucking pests. Aphids, scale and mealybugs secrete sticky honeydew as they feed. In small numbers, these pests can be hard to detect, as they often camouflage themselves or hide under leaves or in leaf sheaths. However, in large infestations, their presence becomes more apparent.

Outdoors, honeydew attracts ants, which farm and protect the pests. Additionally, honeydew promotes the growth of sooty mould, a fungal pathogen that feeds on the sugary substance and coats the leaves with a black sooty powder, inhibiting photosynthesis. While you're unlikely to see ants and sooty mould indoors, it's still possible.

Identifying which pest you have (see pages 28–30) will help you to determine the correct treatment. However, if you can't see any signs or symptoms of pest damage, then it's quite possible that your plant has extrafloral nectaries (EFNs). These are specialised glands that secrete nectar. In the wild, this nectar attracts various beneficial insects, such as ants, which may provide protection against predators. These EFNs can be found on leaf petioles (stems), leaf margins or plant stems, and usually resemble small beads or glands with a glossy surface. Some species of *Philodendron*, *Peperomia* and *Hoya* have EFNs.

Rust

Powdery mildew

Plant diseases

Blemishes and spots on leaves may be signs that your plant is under attack from fungal or bacterial pathogens. Spores, sclerotia or oospores can be present in the potting mix, lying dormant until the right conditions arise to facilitate their growth and potential infection. They can also be blown in or transmitted via sap-sucking pests, such as aphids and spider mites.

Warm, moist and humid conditions are favourable for the growth and spread of diseases, especially when combined with crowded plant arrangements or poor airflow. These factors create an environment where pathogens can thrive, increasing the risk of infection.

Symptoms of plant diseases include:

- necrotic lesions on leaves surrounded by yellow halos
- irregularly shaped brown or black lesions
- water-soaked leaf spots
- poor plant vigour.

Common pathogens affecting indoor plants include:

1. **Rust:** This group of fungal pathogens is characterised by distinctive rust-coloured pustules that typically appear on the leaves. Early symptoms include small yellow or orange spots on the leaf surface; these eventually develop into raised, powdery, rust-coloured lesions.
2. **Powdery mildew:** This fungal pathogen is characterised by a white, powdery coating on the leaves and stems. Initially, small white to grey spots may appear on the leaves; they can quickly spread to cover the leaves. Foliage may yellow and drop.
3. **Bacterial or fungal leaf spots:** These are typically characterised by brown and angular spots often surrounded by yellow leaf tissue.

If just a few leaves are affected, then cut them off at the base of the plant and dispose of the leaves. Ensure that you sterilise the snips or secateurs with alcohol or bleach between cuts to prevent the spread of disease. Fungal leaf spots may also be treated with a broad-spectrum fungicide such as lime sulphur or a copper-based spray.

To reduce the likelihood of future infections:

- Water the soil, not the leaves, to prevent liquid from pooling on the foliage, which creates a damp environment conducive to fungal and bacterial growth.
- Increase the space between plants to improve airflow. This reduces the warmth and moisture build-up that can promote the growth of pathogens. A fan can be beneficial, especially if you're cultivating the plants in an enclosed environment, such as a greenhouse or grow tent.
- Regularly inspect plants for early signs of disease, and remove affected leaves immediately.

White mould on the soil

Fungal spores – the reproductive units of fungi – can be present in the potting mix before they become visible. When there is adequate moisture, warmth and organic matter, the spores germinate and grow into visible mycelia, also known as white mould.

While it's generally not harmful to plants, excessive white-mould growth may indicate overwatering, poor drainage or high levels of humidity, all of which prevent the soil from drying out. Additionally, if the plant is positioned in low-light conditions, then it may not be absorbing water as quickly, resulting in moisture building up in the potting mix. You may even notice mushrooms – the fruiting bodies of the fungi – popping up in the soil.

Reduce watering and/or move your plant to a brightly lit spot, and the white mould and mushrooms will eventually diminish and die off. Improving airflow and allowing the potting mix to dry out will discourage future fungal growth.

Pots

When it comes to choosing pots for your plants, there's a wide range available. I prefer to leave plants in their original black plastic pot, slipping this into a more decorative pot known as a cache pot (cover pot). This approach allows me to change up my display as desired because it's simply a matter of removing and replacing pots rather than repotting plants. It saves time and makes it easier to maintain plants without the hassle of frequent repotting. Plus, I get to enjoy the aesthetic of different decorative pots without compromising on plant care.

Cache pots (cover pots) often don't have drainage holes; if they do, they usually come with a matching saucer that catches the run-off after watering. For pots without drainage holes, be aware that water may pool at the bottom of the pot. A little is usually fine, but if there's a lot, it's best to empty the pot so your plant isn't sitting in stagnant water while it's already moist - this can lead to issues with root rot, and the water may also smell.

Using pots of different shapes can enhance the visual appeal of your indoor garden, allowing you to create interesting arrangements and displays. However, this isn't everyone's cup of tea, so let's look at the types of pots available so you can work out what's best for you.

Types of pots

Plastic
These are cheap, lightweight and readily available. You can re-use them indefinitely if you wash and sterilise the pot between plantings. They're available in a variety of sizes and colours, including self-watering options. However, be aware that colours may fade over time, especially if the pot is positioned in direct sun, and the pots offer poor insulation, so plants may require extra protection in cool or cold climates.

Terracotta
I love the look of terracotta pots, especially when they're grouped together. They provide a uniform, timeless appearance that continues to develop as they age - minerals in water pass through the porous surface, leaving behind calcium and salts that create a lovely patina. Since terracotta is porous, it loses water faster than other pot types, so plants may require more frequent watering.

You can find terracotta pots at affordable prices, and depending on the size, they can range from lightweight to a little heavy. They do become quite heavy once planted, though, so changing up the display can be challenging, particularly for larger pots.

Ceramic
Ceramic pots are mostly available without drainage holes, so this makes them ideal as cache pots (cover pots). There are also options with drainage holes, although the holes are often quite small and not ideal for plants that require good drainage.

They come in a variety of colours, patterns and sizes, offering plenty of choices to match your decor. Unlike terracotta pots, ceramic pots are typically sealed - this means that they are less porous and don't dry out as quickly, so plants won't need to be watered as often.

Self-watering
These pots are a great option if you want to ensure that your plants stay hydrated without the need for constant monitoring. They typically feature a water reservoir at the bottom that allows the plant to draw (or 'wick') moisture as needed and may have a water-level indicator to let you know when the reservoir is low. However, the reservoir is sometimes fairly small, meaning that it needs to be refilled regularly, and these pots may not be ideal for plants that prefer to dry out between waterings.

You may be wondering what the difference is between a self-watering pot and simply sitting a plant in a saucer of water. The key lies in how the water is delivered to the plant. In a self-watering pot, water is stored in a reservoir below the soil level, and the pot only has a few points of contact with the water. This design allows water to be wicked up through the potting mix and reach the plant's roots via capillary action at a controlled rate.

In contrast, when you place a plant in a saucer of water, the roots are often submerged, which can lead to root rot if left for too long. This method doesn't facilitate the same gradual absorption, and the plant might take up too much water too quickly, resulting in overwatering issues. Self-watering pots offer a more measured way to keep the potting mix moist.

Sterilising plastic pots
Remove any old soil and plant debris - these can go into your compost bin or garden beds. Use a firm brush to scrape off any stubborn residue, then wash the pot thoroughly with warm soapy water and rinse well. Let it dry in the sun for natural sterilisation through solarisation. Once dry, spray the surface with eucalyptus oil or white vinegar to disinfect. For a deeper clean, soak the pot in a solution of one part white vinegar and one part water for at least 30 minutes. Rinse thoroughly with clean water, and allow the pot to dry completely before re-using it.

Hunting for houseplants

These days, it's easy to source plants without leaving home. Online plant shops, forums and social groups offer great opportunities to buy or trade plants, and online marketplaces are perfect for finding people who are downsizing their collections or selling propagated plants. That said, it's still worthwhile visiting your local nursery or garden centre, especially since some plants are fragile or too large to post.

Tips for buying plants

Check for pests and diseases
This sounds obvious, but sometimes we're complacent – especially if we see a plant that we've been coveting. Have a close look at both sides of the leaves, stems and leaf sheaths. If the pests aren't obvious, then perhaps their damage is. Are the leaves yellowing, wilted or mushy? Can you feel any sticky residue on plant parts? If so, then these could be signs of pest activity or disease. While it's often possible to treat these issues, the time and effort involved may not be worth it. Worse still, the problem could spread to your plant collection at home. In such cases, it might be best to leave the plant behind and search for a healthier option.

Feel the root ball
Gently squeeze the plastic pot to assess the root ball. If there's some give, then it means that there's still room for the plant to grow. However, if the pot feels overly firm and rigid, then the plant might be root-bound: in other words, it's been in the pot for too long and the roots have encircled the interior of the pot, which can hinder growth. I'd suggest that you look for another plant, but if it's on sale or the last one available, then you can probably salvage it. As soon as possible after you get home, remove the plant from the pot, untangle the roots and repot into a larger container with fresh potting mix.

Decide on the size
A large, established plant can certainly make an immediate statement and add instant drama to your space, without the need to wait for it to grow. You also get the benefit of bypassing the delicate care required to nurture a younger plant to maturity. However, big plants can be expensive and hard to transport or move around, so it's worth considering your budget and space before committing. Remember, small plants will grow into impressive displays with time and patience – and they're a whole lot cheaper, too!

Pet-friendly plants
Some plants are toxic for our furry friends, who are often curious and like to play with or nibble on leaves. It's important to research and choose varieties that are safe for pets.

The spider plant (*Chlorophytum comosum*), the Boston fern (*Nephrolepis exaltata*) and calatheas (*Goeppertia* spp.) are all non-toxic and safe to keep around animals. On the other hand, popular options such as the peace lily (*Spathiphyllum wallisii*), the satin vine (*Scindapsus pictus*) and snake plants (*Dracaena* spp.) can cause stomach upset or more serious symptoms if ingested. Always check for pet safety before bringing new plants home.

Look for the pet-friendly icon on each plant profile in this book – it's a quick way to identify safe options for your space. If you have your heart set on plants that are considered toxic to pets, then it's a good idea to position them out of reach, such as on high shelves, in hanging planters or within enclosed terrariums.

Maintenance

Unlike an outdoor garden, which requires a lot of maintenance, indoor plants just need the occasional tidy-up and perhaps a move into a new pot when they've outgrown their old home.

Pruning plants

As plants grow, they may become a bit unruly. Depending on your available space, you can let them run wild, but if their growth pattern starts to feel too chaotic, then it's perfectly fine to grab a sharp pair of secateurs or snips and give them a trim.

It can be mentally challenging to prune plants, since you've spent so much time nurturing them into happy, healthy specimens. However, rest assured that trimming encourages new growth and often leads to a more vigorous plant overall – so snip away! Plus, you can use those clippings to propagate new plants, or simply add them to your compost or green waste. Remember, you don't have to propagate every cutting.

Repotting plants

When you bring home plants from the nursery or garden centre, there's no need to repot them straight away – unless you absolutely want to, or you found one on the clearance rack that has seen better days.

To decide if your plant needs to be repotted, look out for these signs:

- Roots are emerging through the drainage holes at the bottom of the pot or pushing up through the surface of the potting mix.
- There's little to no give when you squeeze the plastic pot, indicating that the roots have mostly filled up the pot.
- The potting mix is compacted and hydrophobic (water repellent).
- There is little to no new growth, or the plant has poor, stunted growth.
- The plant has become top-heavy, with much more growth above the potting mix than its pot can support.

To repot your plant, you'll need a sharp pair of secateurs or snips, a new pot (one size up), fresh potting mix and a watering-can. Then follow these step-by-step instructions:

1. Squeeze the pot to help loosen the root ball.
2. Slide the plant out of the pot. If large roots are extending through the drainage holes and making the pot difficult to remove, trim them off.
3. Tickle the root ball to loosen the roots, untangling any circling roots and trimming away any dead or damaged sections.
4. Partly fill the new pot with potting mix, position the plant in the centre, and backfill around it. Ensure that the final level of the potting mix is the same as it was in the previous pot to avoid burying the stem or exposing the roots.
5. Lift and tap the pot gently on a surface to settle the potting mix. Add more if necessary.
6. Press down firmly on the potting mix, ensuring that the plant is stable.
7. Water in well, ensuring that the water runs through the drainage holes at the bottom of the pot.

FORGET ME NOT

Hydroculture, semi-hydro and hydroponics

These are alternative approaches to traditional growing methods. Instead of sitting in soil or potting mix, plants are grown in mediums such as lightweight expanded clay aggregate (LECA), perlite or rock wool. Many indoor plant enthusiasts prefer these approaches for their simplicity and ease of management, finding them more efficient for controlling plant-growth conditions.

Hydroculture

Often referred to as 'hydro', this technique involves growing plants in water without any soil or potting mix. The roots are thoroughly washed and submerged, while gravel or pebbles can be used to help keep the plant upright. Water is topped up as it drops, ensuring that most of the roots remain submerged. Changing the water weekly or fortnightly helps to introduce fresh oxygen and prevents stagnation. This practice not only maintains water quality but also supports healthy root growth. A low-dose fertiliser is added to the water monthly to provide the necessary nutrients for the plants to thrive.

It can be a decorative way to display your plants, but personally I'm not a fan of the look! Something about all of those roots floating in a vase of water just doesn't do it for me, but it's not about what I like. If you love it, go for it! I've seen many collections transitioned to 'hydro', and there are even large groups on Facebook dedicated to growing this way.

Semi-hydro

This growing technique involves removing the soil or potting mix from the plant's roots, and potting the plant in a medium such as LECA or perlite, which provides support, aeration and moisture retention – but no nutrients. The pot is placed inside a slightly larger cache pot (cover pot), tray or reservoir holding a nutrient solution to nourish the plant.

The set-up increases oxygen availability to the root zone, promoting healthier roots and reducing the risk of root rot. It's ideal for small, young plants or cuttings; converting large, mature or top-heavy plants to semi-hydro can be more challenging.

For this method, use a fertiliser specifically designed for hydroponics, diluting it according to the manufacturer's instructions. You may also need to adjust the pH of the water (the ideal pH is around 5.5–6.5) because the fertiliser can alter it.

Water the medium until the solution in the reservoir reaches about one-quarter of the pot's height. This allows the medium to wick up water and nutrients, preventing the roots from sitting in water. Top up the solution as needed; every few weeks, remove the inner pot and flush it under running water for a few minutes to clear out excess salts.

Semi-hydro is effective, it does away with a few plant problems (such as fungus gnats and root rot), and plants can be left unattended for a while if you simply overfill the reservoir.

It can be a little time-consuming to convert your plants, but it's time and money well spent.

Hydroponics

This covers a range of different water-based techniques, such as flood and drain, nutrient film technique (NFT), deep water culture and aeroponics. Each system is highly specialised, offering a unique way to deliver nutrients and oxygen to plants. If you're looking to maximise plant potential for breeding or commercial purposes, then it's definitely worth exploring hydroponics. However, for plant enthusiasts, I'd recommend sticking with semi-hydro. It's much easier, less expensive and still incredibly effective.

Going away?

Are you heading off on holiday for a week or two and unsure of what to do with your plants? Some hardy species may not even notice your absence, but most plants will begin to suffer if they're left unattended. Here are five ways to help keep your plants healthy while you're enjoying a well-deserved break.

1. Water plants before you leave
Give all of your plants a thorough watering the day before your trip. While watering on the day you leave might seem ideal, it's often a hectic time with plenty to do. Watering a day earlier means that there's one less thing to worry about, and your plants will still have ample moisture to sustain them during your absence.

2. Group plants together
If you have a bathtub or large laundry sink, then line the bottom with an old towel and add a shallow layer of water to the bottom, just enough to keep the towel damp without letting the pots sit in standing water. This creates a humid microclimate that will slow down evaporation. Arrange your watered plants on top of the towel, keeping them close together to boost humidity.

Even if you don't have a bathtub or large laundry sink to accommodate your collection, grouping the plants together is a good idea. This will increase humidity and slow down water evaporation while you're gone.

3. Move plants away from bright light
Relocating your plants to an area with less light will slow down their water consumption. In lower-light conditions, plants photosynthesise less actively, which reduces the amount of water they draw from the potting mix. However, they'll still receive enough light to maintain their basic functions.

4. Relocate plants from darkened rooms
If you plan to draw the curtains or close the blinds for security reasons, then there will be no light for your plants. Move the plants to a room where there are no blockout coverings on the windows, such as the laundry or bathroom. If that's not an option, then grow lights can help. Many come with built-in timers, or you can connect them to a separate timer to maintain a consistent day-night schedule (such as 18 hours of light and six hours of darkness).

5. Ask someone to plant-sit
Asking a friend or neighbour to water your plants is a reliable way to ensure that your plants stay healthy while you're away. If your helper is a fellow plant parent, then it's likely that they'll already know the drill. Otherwise, it's a good idea to leave clear, detailed instructions on how and when to water. Visual aids (such as labels or photos of your plants) can also help to avoid confusion.

For extra peace of mind, you might consider hiring a professional plant-sitting service. These services either allow you to drop off your plants at their location, or they access your home to care for your plants. While it's an added expense, it's a fantastic option for those with extensive or high-maintenance collections.

If your trip lasts longer than a couple of weeks, then you can expect your plants to show some signs of stress (such as wilting, yellowing leaves or slowed growth) when you return. While your plants will likely bounce back with a little care, it may take some time for them to fully recover.

For extended trips, it's best to call on a plant-sitter to ensure that your plants receive consistent care, especially during the warmer months. A plant-sitter can water, check for pests and even rotate your plants to keep them thriving. Your plants are more likely to stay in good health, and you won't have to worry about them while you're away.

Troubleshooting

As a plant parent, encountering issues with your indoor plants can be both frustrating and perplexing, especially with the varying advice found online. Despite your best intentions – providing sunlight, water and the right potting mix – your houseplants can sometimes show signs of distress. Whether it's yellowing leaves, stunted growth or unexpected pest damage, understanding the root causes of these problems is essential for restoring plant health. Use the flow charts on pages 41–5 to diagnose the problem, then turn to the page number given in the flow chart for detailed information on how to tackle the specific problem.

Wilting plant

Sad, droopy leaves are a common problem for indoor plants. While these are often linked to a watering issue, this may not be the underlying problem.

Yellowing leaves

Yellowing leaves may be the result of several factors, including overwatering, low light or pest damage. It may affect older leaves first and be accompanied by other signs (such as stunted or distorted growth) and overall poor health.

follow to next page

Any signs of distorted growth, sticky residue or foreign bodies on leaves/stems?
Yes
See Pest damage (page 48)
No
Have you fed the plant in the last three months?
No
See Nutrient deficiency (page 48)
Yes
Does the potting mix feel hard or compacted?
Yes
See Potting mix compaction (page 49)
No
Are roots growing out of the drainage holes, or is there not much give when you squeeze the pot?
Yes
See Root-bound plant (page 49)
No
See Hydrophobic potting mix (page 46)

Browning leaf tips or edges

Browning tips or edges of leaves is a common problem for indoor plants. This can occur for various reasons, including inconsistent watering, low humidity or a build-up of salts from overfertilising.

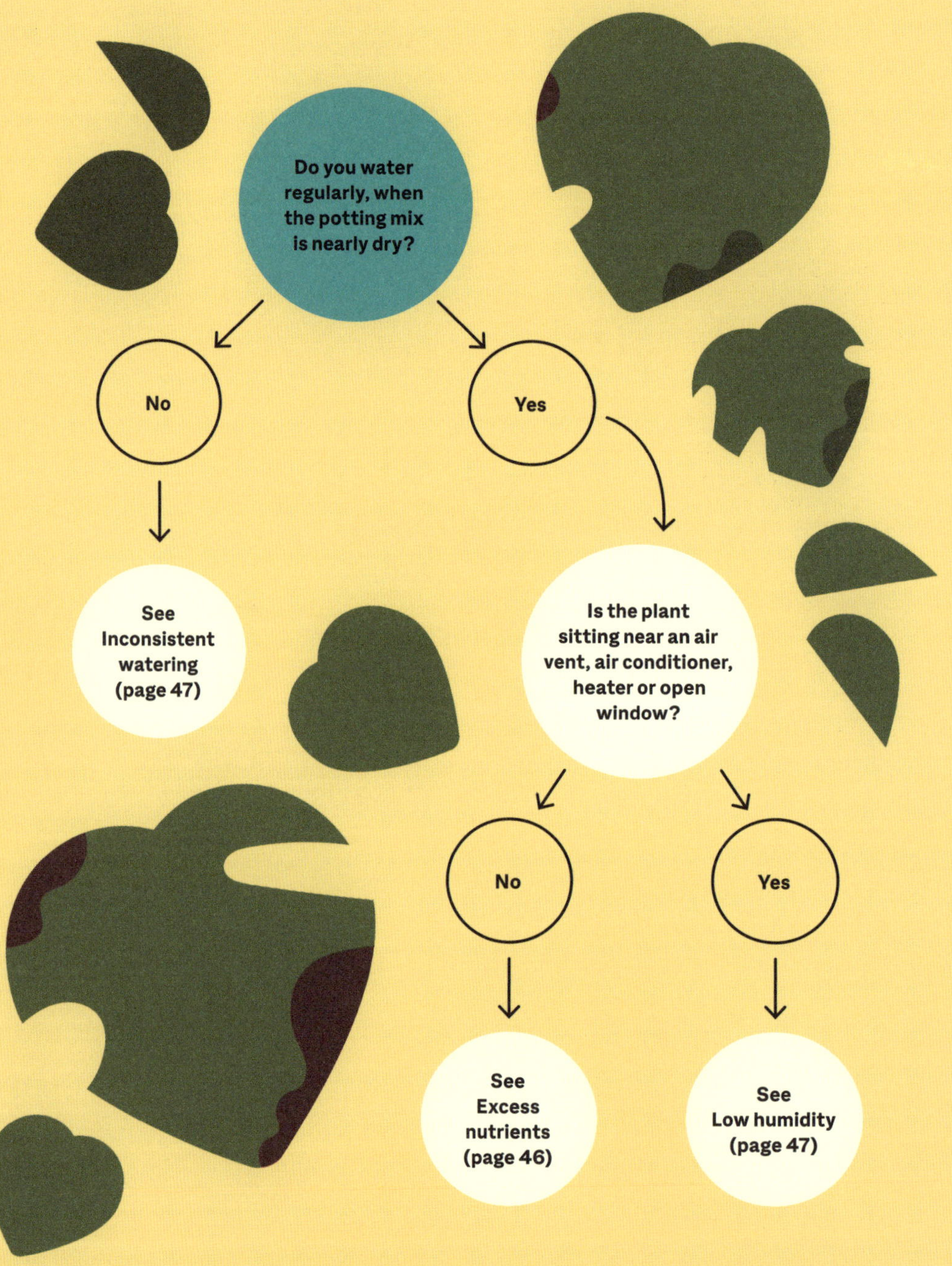

Dropping leaves

Leaf drop is a common sign that a plant is under stress. It may be due to low light or underwatering, or a sudden change in environment. Losing a few leaves is normal, but if a plant is shedding most of its leaves, then it's best to investigate.

Solving your plant problems

Once you have used the flow charts on pages 41–5, here's where you can find out more about the specific problems and – more importantly – their solutions.

Excess nutrients

Have you been a little zealous when it comes to feeding your plant? Overfeeding – whether by feeding more regularly than instructed or by applying more product than required – can cause a build-up of excess salts in the potting mix. The salts can damage the roots, preventing or reducing uptake of water and nutrients, which causes symptoms such as browning or yellowing of leaves and stunted growth.

Flush excess salts from the potting mix by placing the pot under running water for a few minutes. Allow it to nearly dry before watering again. Remove the damaged leaves or cut off the brown parts, and only feed once new growth appears.

Hydrophobic potting mix

Over time, potting mixes can become hydrophobic (water repellent). As organic matter breaks down, it can create a waxy residue that coats potting mix particles, making them resistant to water. As a result, no matter how much you water the plant, the liquid simply pools on the surface; eventually, it runs down the inside of the pot and drains out through the holes. This can create the illusion that you've watered thoroughly even though your plant is still thirsty.

There are three ways to fix hydrophobic potting mix:

1. **Submerge the plant in a bucket of water.** Make sure that the plant and its pot are completely underwater for about half an hour; you may need to use a brick or weight to hold it down. Your plant should perk up within the next couple of days.
2. **Apply a soil wetter or wetting agent.** Available at your local nursery or garden centre, these products help to break up the waxy layer on the potting mix particles. This allows water to penetrate deeper into the mix.
3. **Repot your plant into fresh potting mix.** If your plant is due for a repot – indicated by roots escaping from the bottom of the pot, or not much give when you squeeze the pot – then this is a good opportunity to refresh its growing medium.

Inconsistent watering

When a plant experiences irregular watering – alternating between too much and too little – its roots may become stressed. Overwatering can lead to root rot, while underwatering deprives the plant of moisture. Both scenarios cause the plant to struggle with water regulation, leading to browning leaf tips or edges and/or leaf drop.

Low humidity can make the problem of browning leaf tips or edges worse because it causes water to evaporate from the leaves faster than the plant can absorb it. Together, inconsistent watering and low humidity can amplify stress, but either factor can cause browning on its own.

If the plant has extensive leaf loss, you might consider cutting it back to encourage new growth. Alternatively, an effective technique for plants with woody or semi-woody stems, such as the fiddle leaf fig, is 'notching' the stem – making small cuts into the stem to stimulate leaf growth. For more details, see page 154. (This technique also works for soft-stemmed or non-woody plants.)

Avoid sporadic watering by establishing a consistent routine based on the plant's needs. Check the potting mix moisture regularly, and adjust your watering schedule according to the season, temperature and specific requirements of the plant. If you're short on time (or feeling lazy!), then consider using a device such as a moisture meter (bought from a garden centre) that changes colour when water is needed.

Low humidity

Most of the houseplants we keep come from warm, subtropical or tropical regions. While they can adapt to indoor conditions, if humidity levels fall below what they're used to, then the edges of their leaves may start to brown.

Dry air pulls moisture from the leaves faster than the roots can replenish it. It's best to avoid placing humidity-loving plants near air-conditioning or heating vents, or exposing them to cold draughts or hot winds through open windows. For ways to boost indoor humidity, see page 26.

Low light

In instances of low light, the plant can't photosynthesise efficiently, and it can't produce the energy it needs to maintain healthy growth. It starts to break down chlorophyll – the green pigment in the leaves – leading to yellowing. The plant may also shed leaves to conserve energy as it tries to survive.

Reposition the plant into a brighter spot or under a grow light. Remove the yellowing leaves because they won't recover.

Natural leaf loss

Yellowing and shedding of older leaves can occur due to several factors, such as natural ageing, transplant shock (whether from repotting or relocating), or the plant entering dormancy (for example, in the case of *Alocasia*, *Oxalis* and *Caladium* species). This is normal in most cases, and there's no need to do anything. However, if more leaves begin to yellow and fall, then it may be worth investigating further to ensure that there isn't an underlying issue.

Nutrient deficiency

If you haven't fed your plant since bringing it home – remember, water and plant tonics (such as seaweed solution) are not actual plant food – then it's possible that your plant is suffering from a nutrient deficiency. While a plant produces its own energy from sunlight through photosynthesis, it still relies on essential nutrients from the potting mix to support healthy growth, maintain vibrant foliage and develop strong roots. Without these nutrients, plants can struggle to thrive, leading to yellowing leaves, stunted growth and poor overall health.

Feed your plants during their active growing period, typically in the warmer months, using an indoor plant fertiliser. Avoid the temptation to double the dose in order to make up for missed feedings, as this can cause more harm than good. Instead, follow the manufacturer's instructions, or dilute the fertiliser even further and apply it more frequently, following the 'weakly, weekly' method for a gentler, more consistent nutrient boost.

Overwatering

When the potting mix becomes overly saturated, water fills the spaces between the particles, preventing air from circulating. This suffocates the roots, inhibiting their ability to absorb oxygen, which is essential for healthy root function. Consequently, the roots may begin to rot, leading to a decline in the plant's overall health. The lack of proper root function prevents the plant from taking up necessary nutrients, causing the leaves to yellow.

Overwatering may be the result of:

- watering plants when the potting mix is still moist
- poor drainage, which prevents excess water from escaping the pot
- incorrect potting mix (some mediums retain more water than others).

These situations can all lead to waterlogged conditions, depriving the roots of the oxygen they need to thrive and ultimately resulting in yellowing leaves.

Ensure that the pot has good drainage, and excess water can escape. If the roots are obstructing the drainage holes, then the plant needs to be repotted into a larger container. If the drainage is adequate, then allow the potting mix to nearly dry out and only water again when the top 2.5–5 centimetres (1–2 inches) of potting mix is dry.

If the yellowing is severe and the potting mix is saturated, then it may be best to remove the plant from the pot and assess the roots. Cut away any dead, mushy or foul-smelling roots, and repot the plant into fresh potting mix, ensuring that it's the correct type for the plant.

Pest damage

Scale, mealybugs, spider mites, thrips and aphids feed on plant sap, weakening the plant. This leads to yellowing leaves, stunted growth and distorted plant parts. You may spot the pests on the plant, or signs of the infestation (such as sticky residue on the leaves, or small, black droppings on the underside of leaves). To identify the pests and the methods for control, see pages 28–30.

Potting mix compaction

As potting mixes settle and break down over time, they can become compacted, reducing the space between particles and limiting air pockets. Consequently, plants struggle to absorb nutrients and water effectively. When you water, only a small amount may be taken up by the plant, while most runs out through the drainage holes.

You can loosen the potting mix and improve aeration by using a small stake, blunt skewer or similar tool to poke a few holes into the potting mix. However, this is a temporary solution. You'll need to do this every few months to keep your plants happy.

The best thing to do is to repot your plant with perlite added to the potting mix. I typically blend five parts premium potting mix to one part perlite, but the ratio can vary depending on the plant type. This helps to maintain the structural integrity of the potting mix and reduces the likelihood of compaction.

Root-bound plant

When roots have taken up most of the available space in a pot - often circling around the pot's edge - they become tightly packed, which restricts the plant's ability to effectively absorb water and nutrients. This can lead to stunted growth, yellowing leaves and overall poor vigour.

If you see one or more roots growing out of the drainage holes at the bottom of the pot, or if the pot is plastic and there is little to no give when you squeeze it, then the plant needs a bigger home. Carefully remove the plant from the pot - you may need to cut or break the pot if the plant is stuck - and trim any dead or encircled roots. Gently untangle the remaining roots so they hang loosely. Repot the plant into a slightly larger pot with fresh potting mix.

Transplant shock

Plants at the nursery or garden centre are spoilt with good lighting, warmth and care, which can make the transition to your home quite challenging. Even when placed in a good spot, a plant can take some time to adjust to its new environment. Just as moving into a new home can feel unsettling for us, your plant may experience some stress when acclimatising. This can result in a few leaves dropping as it adapts to potentially cooler or dimmer conditions.

Repotting can also contribute to stress and leaf drop because the roots may be damaged during the transition. After repotting, water the plant with a diluted seaweed solution to help promote strong root growth and to support recovery.

In either case, there's no need to worry too much. Your plant is simply adjusting and will adapt to its new surroundings in time. Many plant parents tend to fuss, moving their plant to a variety of different locations or attempting to repot again and again, but this can exacerbate the problem. Instead, be patient and give your plant some time to settle in.

Underwatering

As the potting mix dries out, the roots dehydrate and struggle to absorb the water and nutrients necessary for plant growth, causing the leaves to yellow and become crispy and fragile. Prolonged underwatering can lead to leaf drop and stunted growth, as the plant attempts to conserve resources to survive.

Give the plant a thorough soaking, ensuring that the water runs through the drainage holes at the bottom of the pot. It should recover over the next couple of days, and you can resume a more regular watering routine to prevent future issues. If the plant doesn't recover, then this may indicate that the potting mix has become water repellent or compacted. For guidance on how to deal with these issues, see Hydrophobic potting mix (page 46) and Potting mix compaction (above).

Plant Profiles and Care

Part Two

Here are 50 houseplant profiles – some of my favourites, as well as others that are commonly grown. Each plant profile includes helpful icons that indicate the level of care required, so you can easily understand what you're in for – whether you're dealing with divas or easy-going specimens – as well as whether the plant is pet-friendly and what the ideal lighting conditions are for best growth.

In the section called 'All the dirt on ...', you'll find key growing tips and care details to ensure that the plant thrives in your home. I've also included a 'Common problems' section, which highlights the most frequently encountered issues for each plant. It has been designed to help you easily identify the problem your plant may be experiencing and provides practical solutions to address it.

Maidenhair ferns

Adiantum spp.

Care
Medium maintenance

Pet friendly
Yes

Light
Bright, indirect light

The delicate nature of maidenhair ferns, with their feathery, lime green fronds on shiny, black, wiry stems, makes them charming indoor specimens. Plant lovers gravitate towards their good looks at the nursery or garden centre, finding it difficult to leave them behind.

Unfortunately, the luscious fronds sometimes start to die back within a week, and many plant parents are eventually left with a pot of sticks, perhaps with a little greenery hanging on. If that's you, then I encourage you to try again with a new maidenhair fern – this time armed with the right care information.

There are over 200 species of maidenhair fern (and even more cultivars), but the most popular include the Delta maidenhair fern (*Adiantum raddianum*) – pictured opposite – and the common maidenhair fern (*Adiantum aethiopicum*), an Australian native. In their natural environments, these ferns are often seen growing in damp, rocky areas, near creeks and in shady woodlands, highlighting their love for moisture.

Have you ever noticed a maidenhair fern growing in the cracks of a wall? Perhaps scowled at it enviously or marvelled in wonder at how it seems to grow with little to no care, while your best efforts result in death? If you look closely, then you'll find that it has discovered a hidden source of water, perhaps from rain or run-off. Moisture is the key!

All the dirt on maidenhair ferns

Light
Maidenhair ferns grow best in bright, indirect light. They enjoy a few hours of direct sun in the morning (avoid the hot afternoon sun), as long as the potting mix doesn't dry out.

Potting mix
Use a specialty fern blend, or mix your own by combining equal parts premium potting mix, perlite or coarse sand, and coco peat.

Fertiliser
Liquid feed regularly during the warmer months, or apply a controlled-release fertiliser at the beginning of spring, reapplying as directed.

Water
Keep the potting mix moist (but not soggy) at all times. If it's allowed to dry out, then you'll notice that the fronds will crisp and brown, even within a day. Use a self-watering pot to help maintain consistent potting mix moisture. Alternatively, sit the pot on a saucer, and top up with water as needed, periodically watering from above to flush out any accumulated salts.

Humidity
Maidenhair ferns are not too fussy about humidity, but it's best to avoid open windows and draughts to prevent the potting mix from drying out too quickly.

Choice species and cultivars of maidenhair ferns

Rough maidenhair fern (*Adiantum hispidulum*)

It's sometimes mistaken for a species of Boston fern (*Nephrolepis*) because of the shape and arrangement of the leaves. But a closer look at the leaflets reveals the classic scalloped edging of *Adiantum* species along the leaf margin. The new fronds emerge blush pink before maturing to rich green.

***Adiantum raddianum* 'Variegatum'**

This is the variegated version of the Delta maidenhair fern (*Adiantum raddianum*), and the white on green makes for a striking colour contrast. Give it the same growing conditions as its green cousins.

Common problems of maidenhair ferns

Crisp, dry, browning leaves and stems

Symptom
Leaves and stems are dry and brown; stems may be completely leafless.

Cause
Insufficient water.

Solution
A few fronds dying back is completely normal, and new fronds will grow to replace them. However, if you notice that the whole plant is dying back, then use a sharp pair of secateurs to cut back the fronds to ground level, water the potting mix, and position the plant in a bright spot, out of direct sun. Water regularly to keep the potting mix moist. Eventually, if your fern isn't too far gone, new growth will appear. (You may have seen advice to burn the dying foliage on the plant. This is because in the wild, after wildfires, maidenhair ferns spring back to life. However, this extreme form of resurrection is not required in the home setting, and cutting back the fronds is sufficient.)

Leaflets yellowing, poor growth

Symptom
Leaflets are yellowing in parts along the frond, with the colour eventually spreading to other sections of the plant. Poor growth may be observed, and there may be a sticky residue on the stems or leaves.

Cause
This is likely to be caused by pests such as mealybugs or scale. Mealybugs look like little pieces of fluff, while scale are small, raised, brown, yellow-brown or white bumps on leaves or stems.

Solution
These pests can be hard to treat because most chemical sprays are damaging to ferns. You can try organic horticultural oils, but spot-spray first and observe after a few days. If the leaves don't shrivel and brown, then proceed with a more widespread spray. With severe infestations, it may be worth cutting back the fronds to ground level and encouraging new growth.

Growing tips

Try terracotta
One of the best maidenhair fern specimens I've ever seen was growing in a terracotta pot, which may seem counterintuitive at first. Terracotta is porous and typically dries out faster than other pot types, which can be a challenge when you're trying to grow moisture-loving plants such as maidenhair ferns. However, the trick was that the pot sat on a matching coloured-plastic saucer, which was regularly topped up with water to provide a consistent supply of moisture. While you could use a matching terracotta saucer, the porous nature of the material means that water may leave unsightly marks on the table, shelf or floor where the plant is sitting.

Normally, I wouldn't recommend leaving a plant sitting in a saucer of water, as this can lead to root rot. But in this case, the combination of terracotta's breathability and the maidenhair fern's need for consistent moisture was the perfect match, allowing the plant to thrive.

Lipstick plant

Aeschynanthus radicans

Care
Low maintenance

Pet friendly
Yes

Light
Bright, indirect light

Looking for a gorgeous trailing plant? Pucker up! The lipstick plant is an excellent choice. Lined with glossy, dark green, oval leaves, the cascading stems spill gracefully over the sides of pots and hanging baskets, adding drama to any vertical space. The emerging red, pink or orange trumpet-shaped blooms resemble miniature lipsticks - hence the common name - and will add pops of colour to your indoor space from spring to summer.

There are patterned and variegated forms, too, as well as cultivars with interesting leaf shapes and textures, offering plenty of variety. Showcase the lipstick plant's beautifully long locks on a high shelf, suspended from the ceiling or displayed on a plant stand.

Native to the tropical and subtropical regions of Southeast Asia, the lipstick plant grows as an epiphyte, using its roots to cling to tree branches and rock faces. If you were feeling up to the challenge, then you could mount it to a board for a unique display. However, I think that it's easier to maintain when it's kept in a pot with a moist, well-drained potting mix.

For a while, I avoided saying the lipstick plant's genus name because I struggled to get it to roll off my tongue. If you find yourself in the same boat, then please know that it's pronounced *esh-kee-nan-thus*. There is your (useless) fact for the day!

All the dirt on the lipstick plant

Light
The lipstick plant thrives in a warm spot with bright, indirect light. It can tolerate lower light conditions, but it won't flower and its growth will slow.

Potting mix
Use a moist, well-drained potting mix. I like to blend two parts African violet mix with two parts perlite and one part horticultural charcoal. I've also seen success with equal parts of premium potting mix, coco peat, perlite and orchid bark.

Fertiliser
Liquid feed regularly during spring and summer, or apply a controlled-release fertiliser at the beginning of spring.

Water
Water when the top 2.5-5 centimetres (1-2 inches) of potting mix is dry. Ensure that the water runs through the drainage holes at the bottom of the pot.

Humidity
The lipstick plant originates from tropical and subtropical regions, so the more humidity you can afford to give it, the better it will grow. Keep it away from draughts, heaters and air-conditioning vents. To increase humidity, group it with other plants. For other ways to boost indoor humidity, see page 26.

Choice cultivars of the lipstick plant

Aeschynanthus radicans
'Curly'

This cultivar has small, dark green leaves that curl inwards towards the stem, making it a fun addition to your plant collection. The unusual foliage provides a fantastic backdrop for the bright red, tubular flowers.

Aeschynanthus radicans
'Thai Pink'

A beautiful cultivar, it has baby-pink flowers and rounded green leaves. Even when it's not in bloom, the trailing stems make for an attractive feature; the plant should be displayed in a hanging basket or on an elevated stand so you can appreciate its handsome foliage.

Common problems of the lipstick plant

Sticky leaves and poor growth

Symptom
Leaves may turn yellow, with stunted or distorted growth. Cottony fluff, or green, yellow, black or transparent insects, may be clustered on leaves and stems, leaving behind a sticky residue.

Cause
Mealybugs or aphids (sap-sucking insects). The sticky residue is honeydew, a by-product of mealybugs and aphids.

Solution
Spray affected leaves and plant parts with an insecticidal soap or horticultural oil, ensuring that the solution makes thorough contact with the pests for effective control. Wipe away dead bugs with a cloth. Alternatively, use a systemic insecticide, which is absorbed by the plant and works from within to eliminate pests as they feed. Repeat as necessary.

Mealybugs

Growing tips

Make use of cuttings
If the trailing stems of your lipstick plant are getting too long, then simply trim them back to the desired length. But don't discard the cuttings - you can propagate them and grow more plants. Remove a few of the lower leaves from the cut end to expose the nodes. Place the cuttings in a jar of water, ensuring that at least two nodes are submerged. If the cuttings are top heavy, then you may want to remove additional leaves from the lower part of the stem.

Top up the water as needed, and replace it weekly to prevent it from becoming murky. Once the roots reach 5-10 centimetres (2-4 inches) in length, transplant the cuttings into a pot filled with fresh potting mix. For a fuller look, you can plant a few cuttings in the same pot.

Chinese evergreens

Aglaonema spp.

Care
Medium to high maintenance

Pet friendly
No

Light
Bright, indirect light

I developed a new-found appreciation for Chinese evergreens when I visited Indonesia while filming with *Gardening Australia* in 2023. We were fortunate to meet with Pak Greg Hambali – fondly regarded as the 'Father of Indonesian *Aglaonema*' – not long before he passed away. He bred close to 100 hybrids, all with strong red or pink tones, because red is highly revered in Indonesian and other Southeast Asian cultures. The time and dedication required to breed a successful cultivar is incredible; it often takes years of careful selection and refinement to achieve the desired characteristics. This makes his work all the more impressive.

The eye-catching patterns on the foliage of Chinese evergreens are particularly striking, with vibrant shades of red, pink, green, white or silver contrasting against lush green. The bushy plants grow slowly to 40–90 centimetres (16–36 inches) in height, so they're ideal desk companions or shelf buddies. Alternatively, elevate them using a plant stand to give them more prominence on the floor.

I've found that, over time, Chinese evergreens can drop their lower leaves. Depending on your perspective, this can either create a long, leggy appearance or give the plant a tree-like shape, featuring a single trunk topped with a crown of vibrant foliage. If you're not a fan of the look, then simply cut back the plant; new growth will reshoot from the shortened stem.

All the dirt on Chinese evergreens

Light
Chinese evergreens thrive in bright, indirect light. While they can tolerate lower light levels, this will slow their growth and can cause the red and pink colouring to fade.

Potting mix
Use five parts premium potting mix blended with one part perlite for drainage. I've also used a blend of four parts premium potting mix, one part orchid bark, one part coco peat and one part perlite. I've found both to be moisture retentive but well drained.

Fertiliser
Feed regularly with an indoor plant or general-purpose fertiliser in spring and summer.

Water
Water when the potting mix is nearly dry. To test, insert your finger 2.5–5 centimetres (1–2 inches) into the mix. If the mix is moist, then leave watering for a few days; if it's dry, then give the plant a good drink.

Humidity
Chinese evergreens are adaptable to the standard level of humidity found in most homes, but they enjoy extra humidity if you can manage it. Group them with other plants, place them on a tray filled with pebbles and water, and keep them away from draughts and air-conditioning vents.

Choice species and cultivars of Chinese evergreens

Aglaonema commutatum
'Pink Dalmatian'

This is such a sweet cultivar! The broad, rich green leaves are splashed with soft pink spots. It's tolerant of medium to low light, but it's best grown in brighter areas to maintain the colouring.

Aglaonema commutatum
'Silver Queen'

A gorgeous statement plant, it has long, narrow leaves that feature striking silver and green marbling. It slowly reaches 30–60 centimetres (12–24 inches) in height, so it can start on the desk or shelf and eventually end up as a floor specimen.

Aglaonema pictum
'Tricolor'

At one point during the rise of indoor plants, this cultivar was valued at several hundred dollars! Thankfully, it's much more affordable today. Widely popular for its distinctive camouflage pattern, the foliage displays various shades of green. This makes it both calming and visually intriguing.

Common problems of Chinese evergreens

Yellowing leaves

Symptom
Yellowing of leaves, which progressively spreads through the plant. Leaves may be dry or have a mushy texture.

Cause
Underwatering or overwatering – although, in most cases I've seen, it's usually overwatering! You'll know that it's underwatering if the potting mix feels completely dry to the touch, while an overwatered plant will have potting mix that remains consistently soggy.

Solution
Give the underwatered plant a good soak, ensuring that the water runs through the drainage holes at the bottom of the pot. Resume a more regular watering routine to prevent future issues.

For overwatered plants, ensure that the pot has good drainage so excess water can escape. If the plant has been in decline for some time, then carefully remove it from the pot and examine the roots. Cut away any dead or foul-smelling roots, leaving only healthy, firm ones. Repot the plant in fresh, well-drained potting mix, and water only when the mix is nearly dry.

Growing tips

Promote bushy growth
Regardless of whether natural ageing or a stressor has caused the lower leaves to drop from your Chinese evergreen plant, it's possible to encourage it to be compact and bushy again.

Grab a sharp pair of secateurs, then follow these step-by-step instructions:

1. Snip off the stems near ground level.
2. Remove any remaining lower leaves from the cut stems, leaving two or three leaves at the top.
3. Place the cuttings into a glass of clean water.
4. Position the glass in a warm, brightly lit spot out of direct sun, and top up the water as needed to keep the nodes submerged. Change the water if it becomes murky.
5. Keep the mother plant in the same spot, and water only when the potting mix is nearly dry.

After four to six weeks, new growth should start emerging on the mother plant, and roots should begin to form on the cuttings. Once the roots are 10–15 centimetres (4–6 inches) long, repot the rooted cuttings into fresh, well-drained potting mix.

Elephant's ears

Alocasia spp.

Care
Low to medium maintenance

Pet friendly
No

Light
Bright, indirect light

Want drama? Elephant's ears deliver! Their bold, sculptural foliage, with a velvety or glossy texture and intricate patterns, demands attention. Often shaped like arrowheads on fleshy stems, the leaves come in rich greens, silvers or purples.

Not surprisingly, given the common name, the large leaves of many species are reminiscent of an elephant's ears. However, some species have more compact leaves in a range of shapes. From towering floor specimens to small desk buddies, there's a perfect plant for every space.

An interesting feature of elephant's ears is that they grow from corms (bulb-like structures that store energy and fuel growth). This explains their winter dormancy. When temperatures drop in late autumn, the leaves may yellow and die back, leaving behind what appears to be an unassuming container of potting mix. But don't worry - this is completely normal. Once warmer conditions return, new growth will sprout from the underground corms. In homes where the temperature rarely dips below 15 degrees Celsius (59 degrees Fahrenheit), dormancy may not occur, and the plant will thrive year-round.

Take care when handling elephant's ears, as their sap contains insoluble oxalate crystals that can cause severe skin irritations. Additionally, avoid consuming any part of them. I've known people who have tried eating them for fun, thinking that, because they're related to taro (*Colocasia esculenta*), they must be edible. However, they are mildly toxic for humans and poisonous for pets, causing tongue and mouth irritation, including stinging and swelling.

All the dirt on elephant's ears

Light
Elephant's ears grow best in bright, indirect light. A few hours of sun in the morning is ideal, with bright surroundings for the remainder of the day.

Potting mix
Use a moist, well-drained potting mix. I like to blend three parts premium potting mix, one part perlite, one part coco peat, one part orchid bark and one part horticultural charcoal; I've also seen three parts coco peat, two parts orchid bark and one part perlite used with success.

Fertiliser
Apply a controlled-release fertiliser during spring and summer. Alternatively, liquid feed regularly during the warmer months.

Water
Water when the top 2.5-5 centimetres (1-2 inches) of potting mix is dry.

Humidity
Elephant's ears prefer a humidity level of 50-60 per cent, so group them with other plants or sit them on a saucer filled with pebbles and water. For other ways to boost indoor humidity, see page 26.

Choice species and cultivars of elephant's ears

***Alocasia cuprea* 'Red Secret'**

This looks like something out of *Alien*, with its metallic sheen and deeply ribbed veins. The leaves start deep burgundy and mature into an iridescent green with a coppery pink glow. Under the right conditions, the leaves can reach 30–40 centimetres (12–16 inches) in length – it's a serious show stopper!

Giant taro (*Alocasia macrorrhizos*)

This species forms an impressive clump, 1.5–2 metres (5–7 feet) in height, with large green leaves that can grow up to 1 metre (3 feet) long. I haven't seen it reach this size indoors (only outdoors), but it's still a striking plant that's perfect for adding bold, tropical flair to any space. There's a variegated form, too, and it's a stunning specimen.

***Alocasia micholitziana* 'Frydek'**

One of my favourites, it has velvety, dark green leaves and contrasting white venations. It remains compact, typically growing 60–90 centimetres (24–36 inches) tall and wide. Place it on a shelf or desk, provided it has sufficient light. It's also available in a variegated form.

Common problems of elephant's ears

Silvery, mottled foliage

Symptom
Leaves have a silvery or bronzed look on the surface. Webbing may be present between leaf edges or leaves.

Cause
Spider mites (sap-sucking arachnids).

Solution
Treat with an insecticidal soap or suitable miticide. Check the label for instructions, and use only as directed. Repeat treatments may be required. Damage on affected leaves is irreversible, but new growth will be unaffected if successfully treated.

Browning leaves

Symptom
Brown leaf tips.

Cause
This typically indicates low humidity. It may be the result of draughts or exposure to hot or cool air, which can dry out the air around the plant.

Solution
Position the plant away from open windows or doors to avoid exposure to draughts. Also, keep it away from heating or cooling vents. For other ways to boost indoor humidity, see page 26.

Yellowing leaves

Symptom
Leaves are gradually turning yellow and dying, especially during late autumn and winter.

Cause
When the room temperature consistently drops below 15 degrees Celsius (59 degrees Fahrenheit), this triggers dormancy in the plant, causing growth to slow or stop until the temperature warms up again.

Solution
The plant is simply undergoing its natural life cycle, so there's no need to be alarmed. In my experience, elephant ears often die back during their first winter, but as they grow and mature, they tend to become more resilient or better adapted to indoor conditions. In many cases, they don't go dormant in future winters.

Growing tips

Propagate your elephant's ears
You can easily expand your collection of elephant's ears by simply propagating them! The plants grow from corms, which multiply naturally around the parent plant and can be separated to grow new plants. During late spring or summer, remove the plant from its pot and gently tease the potting mix to separate the corms from the roots. Fill a pot or tray with a moist, well-drained potting mix, and plant the corms just below the surface. You can also propagate elephant's ears in sphagnum moss or perlite. Position the pot in a warm, brightly lit spot, and water regularly to keep the growing medium moist until the first leaves appear.

Aesop.

Flamingo flower

Anthurium andraeanum

Care
Low maintenance

Pet friendly
No

Light
Bright, indirect light

One of the things I love about the flamingo flower is its vibrant, red, waxy 'flowers' that can last for months. They contrast beautifully with the dark green, leathery, heart-shaped leaves. Interestingly, what appears to be the flower is actually a modified leaf called a spathe, which surrounds the spadix - a fleshy spike that holds tiny, tightly packed flowers.

While red is the most desired and readily available hue, many nurseries and garden centres also stock cultivars in other beautiful shades, such as green, orange, pink, white and dark burgundy.

The flamingo flower is popular for not only its blooms but also its easygoing nature. It's adaptable to various light and humidity levels, making it an excellent choice for a range of indoor environments - and, of course, novice plant parents.

Place the flamingo flower in a decorative pot, and let it stand alone on a shelf or table to inject a pop of colour into the space. If your interior palette is more subdued and minimalistic, then consider incorporating a cultivar with deep burgundy or green spathes for a more subtle accent. Alternatively, pair the flamingo flower with a mix of plants, experimenting with different heights, shapes and textures to create a dynamic and visually engaging display.

All the dirt on the flamingo flower

Light
The flamingo flower prefers bright, indirect light, especially to promote flowering. It can tolerate medium to low light levels, although it may not bloom as frequently and growth will be slower.

Potting mix
Use a moist, well-drained potting mix. I like to blend three parts premium potting mix with one part perlite, but I've also used two parts orchid bark, one part perlite, one part coco peat plus a handful of horticultural charcoal and worm castings or compost if they're available.

Fertiliser
Liquid feed regularly during the warmer months, or apply a controlled-release fertiliser at the beginning of spring, reapplying as directed.

Water
Water when the top 2.5–5 centimetres (1–2 inches) of potting mix is dry.

Humidity
The flamingo flower is generally happy with the standard level of humidity found in most homes. However, if it's placed near windows, draughts or climate-control devices (such as fans or heaters), the humidity may be lower than it prefers. Browning of the leaf tips is often a sign of low humidity. For ways to boost indoor humidity, see page 26.

Choice cultivars of the flamingo flower

Anthurium
'Black Queen'

The dark, moody, burgundy spathes of this cultivar give it an air of understated elegance. It's not as bold as the bright red species, but that's part of its charm. The rich tones complement the dark green leaves beautifully, creating a sophisticated contrast that adds depth to any space.

Anthurium
'Emma'

The rounded, coral-pink spathes of this variety offer a fresh, uplifting splash of colour to any space without being overwhelming. A bright and cheerful plant, it's sure to bring a smile to your face every time you see it.

Common problems of the flamingo flower

Browning leaves

Symptom
Brown leaf tips.

Cause
This typically indicates low humidity. It may be the result of draughts or exposure to hot or cool air, which can dry out the air around the plant and lead to water loss from the leaves faster than it can be replenished.

Solution
Position the plant away from open windows or doors to avoid exposure to draughts. Also, keep it away from heating or cooling vents. To maintain consistent moisture, consider sitting the plant on a tray filled with pebbles and water to increase humidity.

Growing tips

Divide your flamingo flower
As the flamingo flower grows, it produces offshoots – small clumps of plants beside the mother plant. This gives it a fuller appearance, which can be maintained, but if it's becoming too large, then you can simply divide the plant and repot into smaller pots.

To divide your flamingo flower, remove the plant from its pot, brushing away the potting mix to loosen the roots. The smaller plants may naturally separate from the mother plant. If they don't, then identify the clumps and ensure that each one has healthy stems, leaves and roots. Use your hands to gently pry the plants apart. A sharp knife or pair of secateurs may help.

Replant each clump into its own pot filled with a well-drained potting mix, ensuring that the base of the plant is at the same depth as before. Water in well with a diluted seaweed solution, which helps to promote root growth and reduce transplant shock. Place the pots in a warm spot with bright, indirect light.

Crystal anthurium

Anthurium crystallinum

Care
Medium maintenance

Pet friendly
No

Light
Bright, indirect light

A highly sought-after houseplant, the crystal anthurium captivates with its heart-shaped leaves featuring a velvety texture and silver-white venation. New leaves emerge with a coppery brown hue and smooth surface, then gradually mature to reveal the characteristic fuzzy texture, deep green colouration and glittery venation. The stunning foliage makes it a standout in any indoor space, and it's easy to see why plant enthusiasts are drawn to it.

When I decided to buy my first one, it wasn't readily available in nurseries. You could only source it from growers or collectors in the tropics, so I got it via mail order. It was gorgeous! The veins shimmered in the light, and the leaves were so soft. There were lots of 'wows' and 'oohs' in the office, so no doubt you'll have the same reaction when you lay your hands on one!

However, it does require more care than most indoor plants. Native to the rainforests of South America, the crystal anthurium grows on the forest floor or as an epiphyte on tree trunks, so it prefers conditions that mimic its natural habitat: warmth, humidity and a well-drained potting mix. Without these, things can go downhill quickly.

Due to the popularity of the crystal anthurium, enthusiasts have used it to create many hybrids. This has fostered a vibrant online community, where collectors share seeds and knowledge.

All the dirt on the crystal anthurium

Light
The crystal anthurium prefers bright, indirect light. A few hours of morning sun is ideal, with bright surroundings for the remainder of the day.

Potting mix
Use a moist, well-drained potting mix. I like to blend two parts orchid bark, one part perlite, one part coco peat plus a handful of horticultural charcoal and worm castings or compost if they're available.

Fertiliser
Liquid feed regularly during the warmer months, or apply a controlled-release fertiliser at the beginning of spring, reapplying as directed.

Water
Water when the top 2.5–5 centimetres (1–2 inches) of potting mix is dry.

Humidity
The crystal anthurium needs high humidity, otherwise the leaf edges will brown and growth will slow. It likes good air circulation, but avoid directly exposing it to draughts. For ways to boost indoor humidity, see page 26.

Choice cultivar of the crystal anthurium

***Anthurium crystallinum*
'Dorayaki'**

This beautiful cultivar features iridescent silver veins shimmering across dark green leaves. The leaves are more rounded than those of the species; because of this shape, the cultivar is affectionately named after the Japanese filled pancakes, dorayaki.

Common problems of the crystal anthurium

Silvery, mottled foliage

Symptom
Leaves have a silver-bronze appearance. If you look carefully, there are tiny yellow, white or black insects crawling on the leaf. Small black droppings are usually scattered over the surface.

Cause
Thrips (sap-sucking insects).

Solution
Treat with an insecticidal soap or suitable pesticide. Check the label for instructions, and use only as directed. Repeat treatments may be required. Damage to affected leaves is irreversible, but new growth will be unaffected if the insects are successfully eradicated.

Browning leaves

Symptom
Brown leaf tips.

Cause
This typically indicates low humidity. It may be the result of draughts or exposure to hot or cool air, which can dry out the air around the plant.

Solution
Position the plant away from open windows or doors to avoid exposure to draughts. Also, keep it away from heating or cooling vents. To maintain consistent moisture, consider sitting the plant on a tray filled with pebbles and water, or grouping it with similar plants to increase humidity.

Growing tips

Boost humidity
A great way to maintain humidity around your crystal anthurium is to add a layer of moistened sphagnum moss at the base of the plant, ensuring that it reaches right to the stem. As the moss dries, it creates a humid microenvironment that supports the plant. This also encourages the formation of aerial roots along the stem, which can eventually grow through the moss and into the potting mix, helping to stabilise and strengthen the plant.

Bird's nest fern

Asplenium nidus

Care
Low maintenance

Pet friendly
Yes

Light
Bright, indirect light

If you're after a robust fern to grow indoors, then the bird's nest fern is an excellent choice. Unlike traditional ferns with delicate, lacy foliage, it offers a more structured appearance with broad, smooth, lime green fronds that contrast with striking black-brown midribs. These fronds form a deep rosette, unfurling from the centre as the plant matures, eventually creating a bowl-like shape that resembles a bird's nest – hence the plant's common name.

Native to Africa, Asia, India, Hawaii and Australia, this fern typically grows as an epiphyte. It uses its roots to cling to trees or rocks and to absorb moisture and nutrients from the air and rain. Indoors, it doesn't need to be mounted; simply pot it in a well-drained potting mix and place it in a warm, brightly lit spot. While mounting on driftwood or cork is an option, keep in mind that it will dry out faster and need regular watering. Placing the mounted specimen into a paludarium or terrarium will help to maintain moisture.

With a variety of cultivars featuring unique leaf shapes and textures, the bird's nest fern will stand out when grouped with other greenery or make a statement on its own. Since it doesn't spread or grow wildly, it's ideal for smaller spaces – whether that's on a shelf, table or plant stand.

All the dirt on the bird's nest fern

Light
The bird's nest fern grows best in bright, indirect light. It tolerates lower light levels, but don't leave it there for extended periods as this slows its growth and causes its vibrant green fronds to pale. Avoid direct sun because this can scorch the leaves.

Potting mix
Use a specialty fern blend or mix your own by combining equal parts premium potting mix, perlite or coarse sand, and coco peat.

Fertiliser
When the fern is actively growing during spring and summer, feed regularly with a liquid fertiliser that has been diluted to half strength.

Water
Water when the top 2.5–5 centimetres (1–2 inches) of potting mix is dry. Avoid watering the crown or centre of the plant because this can lead to issues with rot. Instead, direct the water towards the potting mix.

Humidity
The bird's nest fern is adaptable to the standard level of humidity found in most homes, although it thrives in higher humidity. To enhance humidity, consider grouping it with other plants or placing it on a tray filled with pebbles and water. For other ways to boost indoor humidity, see page 26. If the air becomes too dry, the leaves may dry out and become crispy.

Choice cultivars of the bird's nest fern

Asplenium nidus
'Crispy Wave'

One of my favourites! The fronds are narrow, pleated and ruffled, and remind me of coral or seaweed. There's something other-worldly about it.

Asplenium nidus
'Crissie'

This cultivar has slender fronds with crested, feathery tips. Its appearance is reminiscent of curly-leaved parsley, adding a unique and playful touch to your plant collection.

Common problems of the bird's nest fern

Small brown bumps on leaves

Symptom
Small brown or coloured bumps on the leaf surfaces (not to be confused with the fern's spores, which are typically arranged in neat rows on the underside of the leaf). They can be easily scratched off with your fingernail. Foliage may be covered with a sticky residue.

Cause
Scale (sap-sucking insects).

Solution
Spray affected fronds with a horticultural oil, such as eco-oil or white oil. Ferns can be sensitive to oils, so it's a good idea to test them on a small, inconspicuous spot. Observe the fern over a few days to see if there are any adverse reactions, such as browning or shrivelling of fronds. Avoid exposing leaves to direct sun while under treatment. If there are no reactions, then you can proceed with a more widespread spray. Alternatively, treat with a systemic product that contains imidacloprid or acetamiprid.

Growing tips

Create a kokedama
A clever way to display your bird's nest fern is to turn it into a kokedama (Japanese moss ball). This involves carefully wrapping the plant's root ball in a specialty mix of bonsai soil and peat moss, shaping it into a ball, then encasing it in sphagnum moss and securing it with twine. The result is a self-contained plant display that can be hung or placed on a surface.

One unconventional method I've used to make a kokedama involves removing the plant from its pot and encasing the root ball in a sheer ankle sock. The sock serves as a simple, flexible casing that holds the potting mix together, eliminating the need to use a specialty mix. I fill the sock with more potting mix, so it covers the roots, then layer sphagnum moss around the outside of the sock, wrapping and securing it with twine until the sock is completely hidden. As you layer the moss, use the palms of your hands to gently shape the ball to achieve a more rounded appearance.

Polka dot begonia

Begonia maculata

Care
Low maintenance

Pet friendly
No

Light
Bright, indirect light

If you're a fan of polka dots, then this is the perfect plant for you. The polka dot begonia features light green to dark green leaves adorned with silver-white spots. As a cane-type begonia, it has upright and semi-erect stems with swollen nodes, and it can grow between 60 centimetres (24 inches) and 1.5 metres (5 feet) in height, although it usually stays more compact indoors.

Unlike its more demanding cousins, the rex begonias (*Begonia* Rex Cultorum Group), this plant doesn't need high humidity to maintain its good looks, making it a hardy and popular houseplant. It's sometimes referred to as an angel wing begonia because its broad, elongated leaves resemble wings. During the warmer months, pendulous clusters of white, red or pink flowers appear, adding even more charm to this gorgeous plant.

The stems can sometimes be a little fragile, snapping off if you walk past them too briskly or if children or pets are playing nearby. But don't worry: those stem cuttings will propagate easily in a glass of water or in a pot filled with propagating sand or perlite.

The stems can have a slight arching habit, giving the plant a graceful, cascading appearance as it grows. If it's too floppy for your liking, then you can use thin stakes and garden ties to help prop it up. Display the polka dot begonia on an open shelf, side table or coffee table, where it works beautifully as a stand-alone specimen.

All the dirt on the polka dot begonia

Light
The polka dot begonia grows best in bright, indirect light or filtered light. Avoid direct sun because this can burn the leaves.

Potting mix
Blend equal parts premium potting mix, compost and perlite. There are various potting mix recipes online, so see what works best for you (or use whatever you have on hand). As long as the mix is well draining and contains organic matter, the polka dot begonia won't be fussed.

Fertiliser
Dilute a liquid fertiliser to half strength, and apply every few weeks during spring and summer. Alternatively, apply a slow-release fertiliser at the beginning of spring.

Water
Allow the potting mix to become nearly dry before watering.

Humidity
The polka dot begonia is adaptable to the standard level of humidity found in most homes. If the humidity dips too low, then the leaf edges will start to dry and brown. To maintain a stable environment, it's best to avoid placing the plant near heaters or air-conditioning vents.

Choice cultivar of the polka dot begonia

Begonia maculata **'Wightii'**

One of the most popular indoor begonias, it has dark green leaves with silver-white spots and a striking burgundy underside. The spots on this cultivar are more prominent than those of the species, which I think adds to its appeal.

Common problems of the polka dot begonia

Coloured patches on leaves

Symptom
White to greyish powdery spots or patches on the surface of leaves, which may eventually leave behind reddish-brown blotches.

Cause
Powdery mildew (a fungal disease).

Solution
Remove the worst-affected leaves, and treat the plant with an appropriate fungicide. Look for products containing active ingredients such as myclobutanil, lime sulphur or potassium bicarbonate. Make sure there's plenty of space around the plant to help airflow and to stop the powdery mildew from coming back.

Growing tips

Propagate your polka dot begonia
The best time to do this is during the warmer months, when the plant is actively growing. You can propagate the plant during other times of the year, but the cuttings may take longer to root.

Start by selecting a healthy stem with at least two nodes, and cut it just below a node using a sharp pair of secateurs. Remove the lower leaves, keeping one or two at the top. Now you have two choices:

1. **Water propagation**
   Place the stem in a jar of clean water and ensure that at least one node is submerged. Position the jar in a warm spot with bright, indirect light, and top up the water as needed to keep the node submerged. Change the water weekly to prevent it from becoming murky or stagnant. Roots should begin to form within four weeks.
2. **Potting mix propagation**
   Dip the cut end in a rooting hormone and plant it in a pot filled with a well-drained potting mix. Water lightly, and cover the pot with a clear plastic bag or cloche to create a humid environment, removing the cover periodically to allow for airflow. Position the pot in bright, indirect light, and keep the potting mix slightly moist.

FRESH FRUITS

Rex begonias

Begonia Rex Cultorum Group

Care
Medium to high maintenance

Pet friendly
No

Light
Bright, indirect light

If any plants deserve the title of 'show-offs', then it's the rex begonias. These stunning plants are specifically bred for their incredible foliage, showcasing vibrant patterns and rich colour combinations, including shades of green, silver, pink, burgundy and purple. This gorgeously gaudy display sets them apart from other types of begonias, such as tuberous, shrub, semi-tuberous, rhizomatous, cane-like and thick-stemmed varieties.

Rex begonias typically grow from thickened underground rhizomes (root-like stems), which store nutrients and moisture, and they have sturdy, fleshy stems that support broad, heart- or shell-shaped leaves. The leaves often have a ruffled or scalloped edge plus a textured surface that can feel pebbly, silky, velvety or crepey. Many forms exude a subtle iridescent sheen. No wonder these are popular indoor plants!

These highly decorative divas come with a personality to match. They thrive in humid conditions and need careful attention when it comes to watering, which has given them a bad rap among plant enthusiasts. However, if you meet their needs, then they'll shine brightly. Plus, they're surprisingly easy to propagate through leaf or stem cuttings.

Rex begonias are hybrids derived from the wild species *Begonia rex*, which is native to the tropical and subtropical forests of Vietnam, north-eastern India and southern China, where it thrives in humid conditions under dappled light. The hybrid plants typically grow to 30–50 centimetres (12–20 inches) in height, and they're fabulous for plant stands, side tables and desks. One of my favourite ways to display them is in terrariums – these containers help to maintain the humidity that these plants love.

While rex begonias do produce flowers, the blooms are relatively small and insignificant, especially when compared with their dramatic foliage. You can remove the flowers if you wish to redirect the plant's energy away from flowering and seed production.

All the dirt on rex begonias

Light

Rex begonias grow best in bright, indirect light or filtered light. Avoid direct sun because this can burn the leaves.

Potting mix

Use a moist, well-drained potting mix, such as two parts premium potting mix blended with one part perlite and one part coco peat.

Fertiliser

Dilute a liquid fertiliser to quarter strength, and apply every few weeks during spring and summer.

Water

Allow the potting mix to become nearly dry before watering. Rex begonias are prone to root rot, so take care not to overwater them. Also, don't wet the foliage because this can encourage fungal problems. In winter, depending on how cold it gets in your home, rex begonias may lose their leaves and go dormant. Water sparingly during winter, and the rhizomes will reshoot once the weather warms.

Humidity

Rex begonias enjoy high humidity. They can tolerate less, but leaf edges may start to brown and crisp. Avoid placing the plants near air conditioners and heaters. To increase humidity, place pots on a tray filled with pebbles and water. For other ways to boost indoor humidity, see page 26.

Choice cultivars of rex begonias

Begonia
'Escargot'

This rex begonia lives up to its name – each leaf resembles a snail! The leaves coil inwards, mirroring a snail's shell, and feature an eye-catching mix of dark green, silver and sometimes purple or burgundy shades. The colour contrast beautifully highlights the spiral effect.

Begonia
'Fireworks'

If you're looking for the perfect statement piece, then this plant delivers in spades. Its large, velvety leaves shimmer with bold shades of burgundy and silver, while elegantly ruffled edges add a touch of dramatic texture.

Begonia
'Kotobuki'

The leaves of this gorgeous plant start off with a pinkish-reddish hue then gradually mature to silver accented by a contrasting dark centre. This unique characteristic allows the plant to have both pink and silver leaves simultaneously, creating a striking display as a stand-alone feature plant or when paired with a lush, green backdrop.

Common problems of rex begonias

Drooping stems and dry leaves

Symptom
Stems are drooping and limp, often accompanied by leaves that are drying around the edges.

Cause
Underwatering or low humidity.

Solution
Avoid letting rex begonias completely dry out. Allow the potting mix to become nearly dry before watering; in other words, only water when the top 2.5–5 centimetres (1–2 inches) of potting mix feels dry. Depending on the degree of wilting, the drooping stems may perk up again within a few days. If they don't recover, then it's best to trim them off with a sharp pair of secateurs.

If the humidity dips too low, then stems may droop and leaf edges may brown. It's best to keep plants in a humid environment to maintain healthy growth. For ways to boost indoor humidity, see page 26.

Small, dark grey spots on leaves

Symptom
Small, dark grey spots appear on the leaf surfaces, displaying a powdery texture. These spots may be closely spaced and can coalesce, creating larger affected areas. Leaves may dry and shrivel.

Cause
Powdery mildew (fungal disease).

Solution
Remove the worst-affected leaves, and treat the plant with an appropriate fungicide. Look for products containing active ingredients such as myclobutanil, lime sulphur or potassium bicarbonate. While rex begonias thrive in high humidity, it's important to ensure that there's good ventilation around the plants; avoid placing them too close to other plants.

Growing tips

How to propagate rex begonias
Rex begonias are fun to propagate because they can sprout new plants from just a single leaf! There are two ways to do it:

1. **Stem cutting**
   Select a healthy leaf, and cut it off at the base of the stem. Trim the stem to about 2.5 centimetres (1 inch) in length, and insert it into a pot or tray filled with a propagating mix (a blend of one part general potting mix and one part perlite or washed river sand) or a 50:50 blend of coco peat and perlite. Position the cutting so the leaf sits just above the potting mix level. To encourage root growth, cover the cutting with a plastic bag or a cloche to create a humid environment. Place the pot in a warm, brightly lit spot out of direct sun, and water regularly to keep the growing medium slightly moist.
2. **Leaf cutting**
   Snip a healthy leaf at the base of the stem, and remove the stem entirely. Turn the leaf upside down, and use a sharp knife to make small incisions along the major veins. Place the leaf right side up on top of a pot or tray filled with propagating mix. Secure the leaf to the mix with pins, U-shaped pieces of flexible wire or small pebbles. Over time, tiny plants will emerge from the cuts along the veins. These can be separated into individual plants or kept together and potted up as a cluster.

Angel wings

Caladium spp.

Care
Medium to high maintenance

Pet friendly
No

Light
Bright, indirect light

Most angel wings in cultivation are cultivars derived from heart of Jesus (*Caladium bicolor*). With over 1000 named cultivars, these plants boast bold, vibrant hues and striking venation. They come in an incredible array of patterns - mottled, speckled and splashed - with combinations of red, pink, green and white on delicate, heart-shaped leaves. Each cultivar showcases its own unique design, so why not grow more than one?

Native to the tropical regions of South America, angel wings thrive in warm, humid environments, naturally growing in the understorey of forests. In a home, they need similar warmth and humidity to maintain their stunning foliage. As temperatures drop in late autumn, angel wings begin to yellow and die back, entering dormancy for the winter. In warmer climates, they may not die back entirely, although their growth slows.

Angel wings die back to a tuberous corm (a potato-like bulb beneath the potting mix). In cooler and temperate climates, it's best to lift the corms from the potting mix, shake off any remaining mix, and let them air-dry in a cool, well-ventilated space for a couple of weeks. After drying, gently remove any roots and stems, then store the corms in a cool, dark place (such as a cardboard box or paper bag) until they're ready to be replanted in early to mid-spring.

In warmer areas, you can leave the corms in their pots over winter. Just keep the potting mix dry until new growth emerges in spring.

Angel wings typically grow 30–60 centimetres (12–24 inches) tall. This makes them perfect for shelves, desks or side tables, where their stunning foliage can be admired at all times.

All the dirt on angel wings

Light
Angel wings thrive in bright, indirect light. A few hours of direct sun in the morning is ideal, but the surroundings should be bright for the remainder of the day.

Potting mix
Use a moist, well-drained potting mix. You can blend equal parts premium potting mix, coco peat, perlite and orchid bark.

Fertiliser
Liquid feed regularly during the warmer months, or apply a controlled-release fertiliser at the beginning of spring, reapplying as directed.

Water
Water when the top 2.5–5 centimetres (1–2 inches) of potting mix is dry.

Humidity
Angel wings need high humidity. Place the pot on a tray or saucer filled with pebbles and water, or group plants together to raise the humidity. For other ways to boost indoor humidity, see page 26.

Choice species and cultivars of angel wings

Caladium bicolor
'Pink Symphony'

Can you ever go wrong with a pink and green combination? The leaves on this stunning cultivar feature various shades of pink, beautifully accented by deep green veins.

Caladium bicolor
'Strawberry Star'

A gorgeous cultivar, it has predominantly pale green to white leaves highlighted by dark green veins and delicate pink specks. Leaves can also emerge with a soft pink flush, offering a beautiful two-tone effect on a single plant.

Caladium praetermissum
'Hilo Beauty'

This cultivar has large, heart-shaped leaves with pale green markings that contrast beautifully with the dark green background. The irregular patterns give it a camouflage-like appearance, although it certainly won't blend in!

Common problems of angel wings

Yellowing, limp foliage and stems

Symptom
Stems and foliage become yellow and limp, particularly in the cooler months.

Cause
The plant is preparing for dormancy.

Solution
Don't panic, your plant isn't dying! It's simply going dormant for winter. Allow the foliage to die back naturally, as the energy is being stored in the corms for the next season's growth. You can either lift and store the corms or leave them in the pot to overwinter.

Growing tips

Clean the leaves
Keep the plant looking its best by dusting the leaves periodically with a damp microfibre cloth. Don't worry about polishing it with milk or some other internet 'hack' – water works perfectly fine. If there's a thick layer of dust, then you may want to consider dry-wiping first before going over the leaf with a damp cloth.

Chain of hearts

Ceropegia linearis subsp. *woodii* (syn. *Ceropegia woodii*)

Care
Low maintenance

Pet friendly
Yes

Light
Bright, indirect light

One of the world's sweetest plants, the chain of hearts has fleshy, green, heart-shaped leaves with delicate silvery patterns and a light pink-purple underside. Its trailing vines drape elegantly over the sides of pots or hanging baskets, making it an ideal plant for shelves or elevated spaces. If the vines grow too long for your liking, then you can simply cut them back or gently coil them around a trellis or a decorative support - such as a wire heart or circle - to create a charming display while keeping the plant tidy.

An interesting feature of the chain of hearts is the small, bead-like structures with a cracked appearance that can be found along the vine - these are tubers. They may also be present in the potting mix or at the base of the plant. These tubers store vital nutrients, allowing the plant to tolerate dry periods. Additionally, they are useful for propagation, as new plants can be grown from these tubers when they are planted in potting mix.

The chain of hearts is a relatively fast grower, with vines typically extending a few metres in optimum conditions. Occasionally, you may even see blooms on mature plants. The tubular flowers look like lanterns, and are yet another charming feature of this delightful plant.

All the dirt on the chain of hearts

Light
The chain of hearts grows best in bright, indirect light or filtered light. It can tolerate lower light levels, but the leaves will soon become pale.

Potting mix
Use a free-draining potting mix, such as one made for cacti and succulents.

Fertiliser
The chain of hearts isn't a hungry plant. A weak solution (half strength) of liquid fertiliser once a month during spring and summer is sufficient. For a more hands-off approach, apply a controlled-release fertiliser specially formulated for succulents at the beginning of spring.

Water
Allow most of the potting mix to dry out before watering.

Humidity
The chain of hearts is adaptable to the standard level of humidity found in most homes.

Choice cultivar of the chain of hearts

***Ceropegia linearis* subsp. *woodii* 'Variegata'**

A gorgeous specimen, it has the classic green, heart-shaped leaves with silvery patterning, beautifully mottled with shades of cream and pink.

Common problems of the chain of hearts

Bare top

Symptom
The top of the pot looks sparse. There are a few vines, but bare patches of potting mix are visible.

Cause
This may be due to older vines losing their leaves as they age, or insufficient light. Alternatively, there may only have been a few vines in the pot to start with.

Solution
This isn't necessarily a problem, but a bare top can look unsightly. To fill in the pot, snip a few lengths from the existing vines and insert the cut ends into the potting mix to encourage rooting and new growth. Alternatively, gently untangle some of the existing vines, and wrap them around the top of the pot. Secure them with pins to help them root and create a fuller appearance. If there are tubers along the vines, plant them into the pot, too.

White fluff and sticky leaves

Symptom
Soft, white tufts resembling cotton appear in leaf joints and along stems, with a sticky residue on the leaves.

Cause
Mealybugs (sap-sucking insects). The sticky residue is honeydew, a by-product of mealybugs.

Solution
Spray affected plant parts with an insecticidal soap. This is a contact insecticide, so ensure that the pests are thoroughly covered for effective control.

Growing tips

Propagate your chain of hearts
Like most succulents, the chain of hearts is easy to grow from cuttings. If the vines are long, then simply take cuttings from the ends; otherwise, cut a few vines from the base of the plant. Remove the lower leaves on the cut end to expose the nodes; this is where the roots will form.

You can propagate the cuttings in either water or potting mix. If you're using water, then place the cuttings in a glass, ensuring that the nodes are submerged, and top up the water as needed. Alternatively, plant the cuttings in cacti and succulent mix, ensuring that the nodes are buried. Water lightly, and place the cuttings in a warm spot with bright, indirect light.

Spider plant

Chlorophytum comosum

Care
Low maintenance

Pet friendly
Yes

Light
Bright, indirect light

The spider plant is a tried-and-true performer. Its narrow, sword-shaped leaves arch gracefully, cascading down like a living fountain. As it matures, the plant produces pups that dangle from the mother plant on long stems and resemble little spiders - giving the plant its common name. Pot up the plant in a hanging basket or place it on a plant stand to get the full effect! If the plant becomes too voluminous for your liking, or you want to propagate more spider plants, then simply cut off the pups and discard them or plant them into individual pots.

Its easygoing nature won me over, as it grows into a lush, vibrant specimen with minimal effort. After a few years of growth, it becomes even more stunning - especially when it has lots of pups hanging below the mother plant. If you're seeking a low-maintenance plant, then this is an excellent choice.

It can tolerate being slightly root-bound, so you don't need to repot it often. Apparently, this practice encourages the mother plant to produce more pups. But don't let the plant become too cramped in the pot because this can affect its growth and health.

The spider plant has a bad reputation for becoming weedy. Its prolific pups can spread quickly and take root, so it's best to keep it contained in a pot rather than plant it outside in the garden - unless you're able to keep it under control.

All the dirt on the spider plant

Light
The spider plant does best in bright, indirect light but can tolerate lower light levels.

Potting mix
Use a premium potting mix. You can add perlite to help maintain the integrity of the mix and prevent compaction, if desired. Blend three parts premium potting mix with one part perlite.

Fertiliser
Liquid feed regularly during the warmer months, or apply a controlled-release fertiliser at the beginning of spring, reapplying as directed.

Water
Water when the top 2.5–5 centimetres (1–2 inches) of potting mix is dry. Ensure that the water runs through the drainage holes at the bottom of the pot.

Humidity
The spider plant isn't too fussy about humidity; the typical level within a home is generally sufficient. However, if the air is drier than usual because of climate-control devices or draughts, then the tips of the leaves may turn brown. If this happens, then simply trim off the brown tips and move the plant to a location away from the drying winds or devices.

Choice cultivars of the spider plant

Chlorophytum comosum
'Bonnie'

You know how running scissors along a ribbon makes it curl? That's what 'Bonnie' reminds me of - a bunch of variegated green and white ribbons, elegantly curled. It's so adorable, and definitely worth buying if you want something different from the traditional form.

Chlorophytum comosum
'Variegatum'

This cultivar is the one you'll commonly spot in plant nurseries and garden centres. It features long, narrow, green leaves with a pale green to white stripe running through the centre.

Common problems of the spider plant

Yellowing leaves, poor growth

Symptom
Yellowing leaves and stunted growth; its overall appearance may be droopy or sad.

Cause
It's highly likely that the plant is root-bound. As the roots outgrow the pot, they become crowded and tangled. This limits the plant's access to air, water and nutrients, essentially starving the plant.

Solution
Remove the plant from its pot, and tease out the roots. Repot it into a larger container with fresh premium potting mix.

Growing tips

Propagate your spider plant
If your mother plant has pups with fleshy roots at the base, then you can grow these into full-sized plants. Snip off the pups from the mother plant, and place them all into a jar of water, ensuring that the roots are under the water's surface. Once the roots are 5–10 centimetres (2–4 inches) in length, you can plant the pups into individual pots or all in one large container. The pups can also be cut off the mother plant and then planted directly into premium potting mix; the roots will quickly grow. With minimal care, these pups will soon develop into healthy, thriving plants.

Never never plants

Ctenanthe spp.

Care
Low maintenance

Pet friendly
Yes

Light
Bright, indirect light

The reason for the common name, never never plants, is unclear. Maybe they never fail to look good? Regardless, it makes for a fun name!

Never never plants often fly under the radar of indoor plant enthusiasts, who typically opt for their flashier relatives - calatheas (*Goeppertia* spp.), prayer plants (*Maranta* spp.) and stromanthes (*Stromanthe* spp.). While their long, oval, patterned leaves are more subtle, they make up for it by being more resilient during dry periods and less sensitive to lower humidity levels. They are much lower maintenance than their more delicate relatives.

One fascinating aspect of never never plants is their nocturnal behaviour: the leaves fold up at night and open again during the day, in a process called nyctinasty, which is also seen in other members of the Marantaceae family. You'll often hear the leaves rustle - it can be unnerving at first, especially in the middle of the night, but you become accustomed to it.

Never never plants can grow between 30 centimetres (12 inches) and 1 metre (3 feet) tall, with the larger specimens having quite an impact in any room. However, if you're short on space or prefer something more compact but equally eye-catching, then there are smaller cultivars that will be perfect for desks, display stands or coffee tables.

All the dirt on never never plants

Light
Never never plants do best in bright, filtered light. They can grow in medium light, but the colouring on the leaves may fade.

Potting mix
Use a moist, well-drained potting mix. I like to combine one part premium potting mix with one part coco peat and one part perlite.

Fertiliser
Liquid feed regularly during the warmer months or apply a controlled-release fertiliser at the beginning of spring, reapplying as directed.

Water
Water when the top 2.5–5 centimetres (1–2 inches) of potting mix is dry. Ensure that the water runs through the drainage holes at the bottom of the pot. Extended periods of dryness can result in curled, crispy, brown leaves; snip them off at the base if they become unsightly.

Humidity
Never never plants prefer humidity to be around 50–70 per cent, although they'll tolerate lower levels. Avoid placing them in draughty areas or near climate-control devices such as air-conditioning vents or heaters, otherwise the humidity will dip too low and the leaf edges will start to brown. For ways to boost indoor humidity, see page 26.

Choice species and cultivars of never never plants

Fishbone prayer plant (*Ctenanthe burle-marxii*)

This species is a reliable performer. It's much loved for its dark green, fishbone patterning, compact size and easygoing nature. Use it to create a bold contrast with other green-leaved plants.

***Ctenanthe lubbersiana* 'Golden Mosaic'**

This stunning cultivar has glossy, green leaves with bands of bright yellow that form a mosaic-like pattern. It can grow up to 1 metre (3 feet) tall and brings a dynamic pop of colour to your indoor plant displays.

***Ctenanthe setosa* 'Grey Star'**

One of the larger cultivars, reaching a height of 1–1.5 metres (3–5 feet), this plant makes a striking statement when fully grown. The leaves are grey-green with distinct herringbone patterning and a purple underside. Although I've found it to be prone to mealybugs, don't let that discourage you - its vibrant foliage and graceful form more than make up for the extra care needed.

Common problems of never never plants

Curling leaves

Symptom
Leaves curled or rolled inwards (pictured above).

Cause
Insufficient moisture in the potting mix causes the leaves to roll inwards to conserve moisture.

Solution
Water when the top 2.5–5 centimetres (1–2 inches) of potting mix is dry.

Browning leaves

Symptom
Brown leaf edges or tips.

Cause
This is often a sign of low humidity. When the plant is exposed to draughts or hot or cool air, moisture is lost from the leaves faster than it can be replaced by the roots.

Solution
Position the plant away from open windows or doors, or any sources of draughts. Additionally, keep it clear of heating or cooling vents. For ways to boost indoor humidity, see page 26.

White fluff and sticky leaves

Symptom
Soft, white tufts resembling cotton often appear on leaves, in leaf joints and along stems; a sticky residue may be present.

Cause
Mealybugs (sap-sucking insects). The sticky residue is honeydew, a by-product of mealybugs.

Solution
Spray affected plant parts with an insecticidal soap. This is a contact insecticide, so ensure that the pests are thoroughly covered for effective control. Repeat sprays may be needed, especially with severe infestations.

Small bumps on leaves

Symptom
Small, creamy white to brown bumps on leaves and/or stems. They can be scratched off with your fingernail.

Cause
Scale (sap-sucking insects).

Solution
Spray the plant with a horticultural oil, such as eco-oil or white oil. This contact insecticide must smother the pests to be effective. However, this can be challenging, as scale insects often hide in leaf sheaths, making detection difficult. In such cases, consider using a systemic product that contains imidacloprid or acetamiprid for more comprehensive control. The scale will eventually drop off or can be wiped away with a damp microfibre cloth.

Growing tips

Propagate your never never plant
If your plant has reached its mature size and needs repotting, but space constraints prevent moving up to a larger pot, then consider dividing the plant and repotting the sections into smaller containers.

Grab a clean, sharp pair of secateurs or an old bread knife, then follow these step-by-step instructions:

1. Remove the plant from its pot, and use your fingers to gently tease the potting mix away from the roots.
2. Using secateurs or the bread knife, divide the plant in half by cutting through the roots. Make sure that each division has sufficient undamaged roots.
3. Repot the divisions into fresh potting mix, and water in well.

FRED GREGORY

String of pearls

Curio rowleyanus (syn. *Senecio rowleyanus*)

Care
Low maintenance

Pet friendly
No

Light
Bright, indirect light

This sweet succulent has distinctive trailing strands of bead-like leaves that resemble delicate pearls, hence its common name. It looks great spilling over the sides of pots or hanging baskets, so place it in an elevated position - such as on a shelf or hung from the ceiling - so you can fully appreciate its beauty. It is also rather decorative when the stems are gathered together on a horizontal surface.

Native to the dry regions of south-western Africa, string of pearls is tolerant of dry conditions thanks to its pea-like leaves that store water. This clever adaptation allows the plant to survive periods of drought, making it an excellent choice for people who forget to water their houseplants regularly. The unique shape of its leaves, with their small surface area, also helps to minimise water loss, allowing the plant to thrive in dry conditions with minimal maintenance. But this isn't permission to neglect it! While it is low maintenance, the string of pearls will still appreciate a little care to keep it thriving.

Many people mistakenly place the string of pearls in full sun, assuming that it will thrive in direct light because it's a succulent. However, this can cause the foliage to bleach, resulting in a yellowed, sickly appearance. Instead, position it in a location with bright, indirect light, which allows it to maintain its vibrant green colour.

All the dirt on the string of pearls

Light
String of pearls grows best in bright, indirect light. A few hours of direct sun in the morning is fine, but the light should be bright and indirect or filtered for the remainder of the day.

Potting mix
Use a free-draining potting mix made for cacti and succulents.

Fertiliser
Every month from spring to summer, you can apply a liquid fertiliser that has been diluted to half strength. Alternatively, at the beginning of spring, apply a controlled-release fertiliser that has been specially formulated for succulents.

Water
Allow most of the potting mix to dry out before watering.

Humidity
The string of pearls is adaptable to the standard level of humidity found in most homes.

Choice species and cultivars of the string of pearls

String of dolphins
(*Curio × peregrinus*, syn. *Senecio peregrinus*)

This cutie is a hybrid between string of pearls and *Curio articulatus* (syn. *Senecio articulatus*), with the surprising result of succulent leaves that resemble little dolphins. The unique shape of the leaves makes it a whimsical addition to any plant collection.

String of bananas
(*Curio radicans*, syn. *Senecio radicans*)

This succulent has vines with fleshy leaves that are shaped like tiny, green bananas. It will be another adorable addition to your collection!

Curio rowleyanus
'Variegata'

This beautiful variation on the classic string of pearls is distinguished by its delicate green pearls streaked with white and cream.

Common problems of the string of pearls

Bare top

Symptom
The top of the pot looks sparse, with few pearls on vines, and bare patches of potting mix are visible (pictured below).

Cause
This issue is often caused by insufficient light reaching the entire plant, resulting in dieback at the top while the lower foliage remains healthy. In its natural habitat, it grows as a ground cover that receives light evenly on its leaves. However, in a pot or hanging basket, it may not receive the light as evenly.

Solution
Move the plant to a spot with brighter light. To thicken up the top, you can snip a few lengths from the existing vines and insert the cut ends into the potting mix, ensuring that a couple of nodes are buried to encourage rooting. You can also coil some of the existing vines around the top and secure them with U-shaped pins to promote rooting and a fuller appearance.

Wrinkled pearls

Symptom
The pearls look slightly elongated on both sides, with a wrinkled appearance.

Cause
This is usually a sign of underwatering.

Solution
While this succulent can tolerate dry periods, don't let it go too long without a drink. Give it a good, deep soak, and the pearls should plump back up within a few days, provided they're not completely shrivelled and dead.

White fluff and sticky leaves

Symptom
Soft white tufts resembling cotton appear in leaf joints and along the stems, with a sticky residue on the leaves.

Cause
Mealybugs (sap-sucking insects). The sticky residue is honeydew, a by-product of mealybugs.

Solution
Insecticidal soap and horticultural oil are both effective options. However, succulents such as string of pearls can be sensitive to chemicals. It's best to first test these treatments on a small, inconspicuous area of the plant and observe for a few days to check for any adverse reactions, such as burnt foliage or shrivelled pearls. If no negative effects are observed, then you can proceed with a more widespread application. Alternatively, carefully dab a cotton bud soaked in rubbing alcohol directly onto the pests.

Growing tips

Propagate your string of pearls
Propagating your string of pearls is a great way to make your existing plant look fuller or to expand your plant collection. There are two ways you can do this:

1. Take a few cuttings, and lay them on top of a pot or tray filled with potting mix. You can wind them around the top of the pot, or lay them in rows. Water regularly to keep the potting mix moist.
2. Take a handful of cuttings that are at least 10 centimetres (4 inches) long. Remove a few of the beads from the cut end, and place the cuttings in a glass jar filled with water. Top up the water as needed to keep the ends submerged, and change the water weekly to prevent it from becoming murky and stagnant. Transplant the cuttings into a pot filled with cacti and succulent mix once the roots are 7–10 centimetres (2¾–4 inches) in length.

CORREIO

Persian cyclamen

Cyclamen persicum

Care
Low to medium maintenance

Pet friendly
No

Light
Bright, indirect light

I have a soft spot for the Persian cyclamen. Not because I received one as a gift or have a personal attachment to the plant, but because one of the first plant profiles I ever wrote was about cyclamens. Fresh out of university, I landed my first job as the assistant gardening editor at *Better Homes and Gardens* magazine, and one of my earliest assignments was an article called 'How to grow cyclamens'. It was for the May issue, which had a strong Mother's Day focus, and I quickly learned that cyclamens were a popular gift for mums!

However, let's not forget that the Persian cyclamen is a gorgeous plant in its own right. The flowers bloom from autumn to spring and come in a wide range of colours, including shades of pink, red, white and purple. Delicate petals sit elegantly above the decorative, heart-shaped leaves.

The plant typically reaches a height of 15–30 centimetres (6–12 inches), making it perfect for tabletop displays or any indoor setting where you can enjoy both its stunning blooms and its ornamental foliage. To tidy up spent or dead flowers, gently twist them off at the base.

Sadly, many people discard or neglect their Persian cyclamen once the flowers have faded and the leaves have yellowed and died back, revealing the corm (a brown, potato-like structure near the potting mix surface). They mistakenly believe that the plant is dead. In reality, it has entered dormancy, a natural process that the plant undergoes during warmer months to conserve water, just as it does in its native habitat of the rocky, dry Mediterranean region. The corm stores energy for the next growing season, allowing the plant to re-emerge with the right care.

All the dirt on the Persian cyclamen

Light
The Persian cyclamen grows best in bright, indirect light.

Potting mix
Use a premium potting mix. Repot after a few years into a fresh mix, and keep the top of the corm visible to prevent issues with rot.

Fertiliser
Liquid feed regularly during autumn and spring.

Water
Water when the top 2.5–5 centimetres (1–2 inches) of potting mix is dry, taking care to avoid wetting the leaves and corm, as this can lead to rot. Using a narrow-spouted watering-can will help to direct the water precisely to the potting mix. Reduce watering as the plant prepares for dormancy, and stop completely once it's dormant. You can resume watering once new growth appears in autumn.

Humidity
The Persian cyclamen is adaptable to the standard level of humidity found in most homes, but it prefers cool, moist conditions. Avoid placing it in warm, stuffy rooms, and keep it away from heaters or air conditioners because these can dry out the air.

Common problems of the Persian cyclamen

Yellowing, limp foliage and stems

Symptom
Flower stems collapsing, leaves yellowing.

Cause
Overwatering or poor drainage, leading to rot.

Solution
Inspect the corm by gently touching it; if it feels soft, then this may indicate rot due to excessive moisture or inadequate drainage. Unfortunately, if the corm has rotted, then it's best to discard the plant. However, if it remains firm, allow the potting mix to nearly dry out before watering again, and avoid wetting the leaves or the corm. If necessary, repot the cyclamen into fresh potting mix or a pot with better drainage.

Sticky leaves and poor growth

Symptom
The leaves or stems may feel sticky, and you might notice cotton-like fluff on the stems or leaves, or small insects. Leaves may also yellow.

Cause
Aphids or mealybugs (sap-sucking insects).

Solution
Both aphids and mealybugs secrete a sticky substance known as honeydew. Aphids can appear in various colours, including green, brown and black (or be translucent), while mealybugs manifest as white, cotton-like fluff. Both pests can be treated with insecticidal soap. Repeat applications may be necessary if the infestation is severe.

Silvery, mottled leaves

Symptom
The leaves exhibit a dull silvery sheen, and fine webbing may be observed between the leaves and stems.

Cause
Spider mites (sap-sucking arachnids).

Solution
Treat the plant with an insecticidal soap or miticide, such as abamectin. Follow the manufacturer's instructions for application.

Growing tips

Keep your Persian cyclamen cool

The Persian cyclamen thrives in cool conditions, making autumn and winter the perfect seasons to enjoy them indoors. However, if you tend to have the heater on at night - understandable on those chilly evenings - it's best to move your plant to another room or even place it outdoors overnight. Warm temperatures can prompt the plant to enter dormancy earlier than usual, which can affect its flowering. Keeping your plant in a cool spot will help it to stay vibrant and bloom for longer.

Rabbit's foot fern

Davallia solida var. *fejeensis* (syn. *Davallia fejeensis*)

Care
Low maintenance

Pet friendly
Yes

Light
Bright, indirect light

No matter how many times I see it, the rabbit's foot fern never ceases to fascinate me. The brown, hairy rhizomes (root-like stems) grow on the surface and are said to resemble rabbit's feet, but they look more like spider's legs to me!

The rhizomes creep along the top of the potting mix and eventually find their way to the edge of the pot, where they spill over the sides and cover the exterior of the pot. An interesting feature of these rhizomes is their ability to propagate new plants. You only need a small piece to start a new plant, making it a great option for expanding your collection.

The rabbit's foot fern has lacy, green leaves that provide an intriguing contrast to its rugged rhizomes. Native to the tropical rainforests of Fiji, New Caledonia and other Pacific islands, it thrives in warm, humid conditions. If you can replicate these conditions, then you'll have a very happy houseplant.

A great candidate for hanging baskets, it will be content in the same pot or basket for quite a while. Eventually, the hairy rhizomes will envelop the container and make a dramatic visual statement. You could try upcycling an old and unwanted household item (such as a metal colander or saucepan) into an interesting pot for it to take over – just drill four or five medium-sized holes in the base if it's non-porous to allow water to drain away.

All the dirt on the rabbit's foot fern

Light
The rabbit's foot fern thrives in bright, indirect light. Avoid direct sun, as this can burn the leaves.

Potting mix
Use a premium potting mix made for ferns, or blend your own using equal parts premium potting mix, coco peat and coarse sand.

Fertiliser
Use a half-strength liquid fertiliser during the warmer months, or apply a controlled-release fertiliser at the beginning of spring.

Water
Water when the top 2.5–5 centimetres (1–2 inches) of potting mix is dry.

Humidity
The rabbit's foot fern can tolerate the standard level of humidity found in most homes, but it will appreciate a little more humidity if you can manage it. For ways to boost indoor humidity, see page 26. Keep it away from draughts, air-conditioning vents and heaters to prevent it from drying out too quickly.

Common problems of the rabbit's foot fern

Raised lumps on plant parts

Symptom
Brown, black or coloured bumps on leaves and stems. They can be easily scratched off with your fingernail or a blunt knife. The affected plant parts may also be covered in a sticky residue.

Cause
Scale (sap-sucking insects).

Solution
Like most ferns, the rabbit's foot fern is sensitive to chemical sprays. If scale are spotted, then use a cotton bud to wipe them off. If the infestation is severe, then it's best to prune the affected fronds.

Growing tips

Propagate your rabbit's foot fern
Grab a sharp pair of snips or secateurs, then follow these step-by-step instructions:

1. Cut off 5–10 centimetres (2–4 inches) of the rhizome with a leaf attached.
2. Place the section on top of a pot filled with a premium potting mix made for ferns.
3. Secure the section in place with a U-shaped pin.
4. Position the pot in a warm spot, and keep the potting mix consistently moist. Roots will begin to develop in six to eight weeks.

TAA

Dumb canes

Dieffenbachia spp.

Care
Low maintenance

Pet friendly
No

Light
Bright, indirect light

It's not the most appealing common name, but 'dumb cane' is certainly descriptive of what plants in this genus can do if they're consumed. They contain oxalates, which can cause your tongue to swell and lead to intense pain, effectively leaving you temporarily mute or 'dumb'. This natural defence mechanism is a good reason to admire the plants from afar rather than tasting them!

Fortunately, they're handsome plants to look at. There are numerous cultivars available, predominantly featuring vibrant variations of green and white. Many of these cultivars boast unique patterns, including striking speckles, spots or marbled effects, and they range from compact forms to tall specimens, making them versatile for a variety of spaces.

Plants tend to lose their lower leaves as they mature or if they're exposed to insufficient light. This gives them a tree-like quality, where a bamboo-esque trunk is topped with a crown of lush, green foliage. Depending on your perspective, you may see this as quite a statement or think that the plants look sickly.

Native to tropical rainforests of Central and South America, dumb canes grow under the canopy, thriving in dappled light and warm, humid conditions. Their adaptability to indoor environments makes them a popular choice as houseplants. However, caution is essential when handling them, whether trimming leaves or pruning, as their sap is a skin irritant and can cause dermatitis and severe pain. Always wear gloves, and take care to avoid contact with the sap.

All the dirt on dumb canes

Light
Dumb canes thrive in bright, indirect light. While they can tolerate lower light levels, this may lead to taller, leggier stems as they stretch towards the light, and slower growth.

Potting mix
Use five parts premium potting mix blended with one part perlite for drainage.

Fertiliser
Feed regularly with an indoor plant fertiliser in spring and summer.

Water
Water when the potting mix is nearly dry. To test this, insert your finger 2.5–5 centimetres (1–2 inches) into the mix. If the mix is moist, then leave watering for a few days; if it's dry, then give the plant a good drink.

Humidity
Dumb canes are adaptable to the standard level of humidity found in most homes. But if you can increase the humidity, then they'll appreciate it. Group them with other plants, use a humidity tray, and keep the plants away from draughts and air-conditioning vents. For other ways to boost indoor humidity, see page 26.

Choice cultivars of dumb canes

***Dieffenbachia* 'Reflector'**

This stunning cultivar has velvety green leaves marbled with vibrant, irregular patterns of yellow and lime, almost giving it a glow. It's a fabulous choice for adding a touch of drama to your indoor plant collection.

***Dieffenbachia* 'Tropic Snow'**

This classic cultivar features large, glossy leaves with a beautiful blend of creamy white and green variegation. It's a more subtle version of 'Reflector' and a great choice if you're looking for something a little subdued. It offers elegance without overpowering a space.

Common problems of dumb canes

Long, leggy stems

Symptom
Growth is not bushy; instead, it appears sparse, with few leaves concentrated at the top.

Cause
Insufficient light.

Solution
Dumb canes thrive in bright, indirect light. If they're in low light for extended periods, then they may lose leaves and develop a long, leggy appearance. To rejuvenate your plant, propagate the bushy part of the stem by taking a cutting from below a couple of nodes. Place the cutting in water or a well-drained potting mix until it roots. Meanwhile, relocate the original plant to a brighter spot to encourage new growth. With proper care, both the propagated cutting and the original plant can flourish together.

Growing tips

Propagate your dumb cane
There are a couple of ways to propagate your dumb cane. As outlined above, you can cut the stem back to a few nodes, which will encourage new growth on the stem and also allow you to propagate the cuttings. Another effective method is division, which is best done with a large, well-established plant during the warmer months when it's actively growing.

Remove the plant from its pot, and tickle the potting mix to loosen the roots. Have a close look at the base of the plant to identify the smaller clumps. Before separating the clumps, ensure that each one has healthy stems, leaves and roots. Use your hands to gently pry the clumps apart. A sharp knife or pair of secateurs may help.

Replant each clump into its own pot filled with potting mix, ensuring the base of the plant is at the same depth as before. Water in well with a diluted seaweed solution – this helps to promote root growth and reduce transplant shock. Place the pots in a warm spot with bright, indirect light.

PROVIDENCE

Fishbone cactus

Disocactus anguliger (syn. *Epiphyllum anguliger*)

Care
Low maintenance

Pet friendly
Yes

Light
Bright, indirect light

It makes perfect sense to call this plant the fishbone cactus - just look at those distinctive stems! They're actually modified structures known as cladodes, which store water and help with photosynthesis.

This is a fun indoor plant, especially as it grows larger and its succulent stems zigzag wildly over the edges of pots or hanging baskets. It looks best suspended from the ceiling, placed on a shelf or positioned on a tall plant stand, so you appreciate its chaotic, trailing form.

While it belongs to the cactus family, it's not the typical cactus associated with arid deserts. Instead, it's a jungle cactus that grows as an epiphyte in its native Mexico. This means it thrives in humid, shaded environments rather than the dry, sun-soaked conditions typical of desert cacti. As an epiphyte (a plant that grows on another plant), it uses its roots to anchor itself to trees and to absorb moisture and nutrients from the air and surrounding debris. Because of this adaptation, the plant requires consistent watering and a moderately humid environment indoors.

The fishbone cactus lacks the sharp spines found on desert cacti, but it may have a few bristles along the length of the stems. While these bristles can be spiky, they are generally softer and less rigid than cactus spines.

All the dirt on the fishbone cactus

Light
The fishbone cactus grows best in bright, indirect light or filtered light. A few hours of direct sun in the morning is ideal, but the light should be filtered for the remainder of the day. Avoid low light levels, as these conditions will cause the stems to become thin and stringy.

Potting mix
Use a moist, well-drained potting mix, such as two parts premium potting mix blended with one part perlite and one part orchid bark.

Fertiliser
Apply a general-purpose controlled-release fertiliser at the beginning of spring, reapplying as directed. Alternatively, once a month from spring to late summer, apply a liquid fertiliser that has been diluted to half strength.

Water
Water when the top 2.5–5 centimetres (1–2 inches) of potting mix is dry.

Humidity
The fishbone cactus is adaptable to the standard level of humidity found in most homes. The plant will enjoy a little more humidity if you can manage it, but this is not necessary. To maintain a stable environment, it's best to avoid placing the plant near draughts or air-conditioning vents.

Common problems of the fishbone cactus

White, cottony deposits on stems

Symptom
Soft, white tufts resembling cotton are found along the stems, often accompanied by a sticky residue.

Cause
Mealybugs (sap-sucking insects). The sticky residue is honeydew, a by-product of mealybugs.

Solution
Jungle cacti (such as the fishbone cactus) can be sensitive to horticultural oils or insecticidal soap. Try these on a test patch, and check for any negative reactions (such as burning or browning of the stems) over a few days before applying them more widely. Alternatively, carefully dab a cotton bud soaked in rubbing alcohol directly onto the pests. This method targets the infestation while minimising the risk to the plant.

Numerous stringy aerial roots

Symptom
A number of aerial roots develop along the midrib of the stems.

Cause
This is a natural adaptation for epiphytic cacti.

Solution
While the presence of aerial roots may raise questions, they're not necessarily a cause for concern. It's normal for the fishbone cactus to develop these roots, which help it cling to surfaces and absorb moisture and nutrients from the air in its native environment. High humidity can encourage the formation of aerial roots, but they may also appear as a stress response to inadequate watering or low humidity. Understanding the context can help you to determine whether the aerial roots are a sign of healthy adaptation or a reaction to environmental stress.

Growing tips

Strengthen your fishbone cactus
Have you noticed that the new growth on your fishbone cactus seems smaller or skinnier than usual? This is usually due to insufficient light. Remove the thinner current stems, and place the plant in a brighter spot so it will start to produce more robust stems.

Happy plant

Dracaena fragrans

Care
Low maintenance

Pet friendly
No

Light
Bright, indirect light

When I was growing up, there were always happy plants in our home. I never thought much about it at the time - one was by the front door in a dimly lit area, while the other one lived outside on the patio. It wasn't until later that I realised they weren't chosen just for their handsomeness. They symbolise good luck and prosperity, so by placing them around our home, my parents were inviting luck and fortune to come our way.

The happy plant looks appealing with minimal effort. A crown of long, glossy, green leaves, striped pale yellow down the centre, sits atop a thick, corky stem, giving it a tree-like appearance. It's common to see a few stems of varying heights in one pot, which adds to its fullness and visual appeal.

One of the best features of the happy plant is its adaptability. It grows in a range of lighting conditions, from low light through to bright, indirect light, making it a versatile choice for any room. It's also forgiving if you occasionally forget to water it, as it can tolerate some neglect.

If you're looking for a plant that brings both aesthetic charm and perhaps a little luck into your space, then the happy plant is the perfect choice. It makes a great house-warming gift, too!

All the dirt on the happy plant

Light
The happy plant thrives in bright, indirect light. It can tolerate lower light levels, but growth may become thin and leggy as the plant stretches out for more light.

Potting mix
Use a premium potting mix.

Fertiliser
Apply a controlled-release fertiliser at the beginning of spring, reapplying as directed. You can liquid feed instead, if you prefer.

Water
Water when the top 2.5–5 centimetres (1–2 inches) of potting mix is dry. Ensure that the water runs through the drainage holes at the bottom of the pot. The leaves will droop dramatically if the potting mix becomes too dry.

Humidity
The happy plant is fine with the standard level of humidity found in most homes. If the humidity dips too low because of cool or hot draughts, then you may see some browning on the edges of the leaves. Move the plant from the area, or look for ways to increase the humidity. If you find the browning unsightly, then trim it off, following the natural shape of the leaf.

Choice cultivars of the happy plant

Dracaena fragrans
'Janet Craig'

This cultivar has gorgeous, lightly ribbed, dark green leaves. It's tolerant of low light conditions, maintaining its lush appearance. It's a great one for the office!

Dracaena fragrans
'Lemon Lime'

Its long, sword-shaped leaves are boldly edged in bright green or lemon yellow, making a striking contrast with the green centres. Also, it's incredibly easy to maintain.

Dracaena fragrans
'Massangena'

This popular cultivar is known for its handsome green leaves highlighted by a yellow or lime-green stripe running down the centre. It's best grown in bright, indirect light to maintain its thick, corky stem and lush growth.

Common problems of the happy plant

White, cottony fluff on leaves and stems

Symptom
White, fluffy clusters on leaves, stems and joints. Affected plant surfaces may have a sticky residue.

Cause
Mealybugs (sap-sucking insects). The sticky residue is honeydew, a by-product of mealybugs.

Solution
Spray affected leaves and plant parts with an insecticidal soap or horticultural oil, ensuring that the solution makes thorough contact with the pests for effective control. Wipe away dead bugs with a cloth. For severe infestations, repeat applications may be necessary.

Silvery, mottled foliage

Symptom
Leaves develop a silvery, mottled appearance, and fine webbing may be observed between the leaves and stems.

Cause
Spider mites (sap-sucking arachnids).

Solution
Spray the plant with an insecticidal soap or horticultural oil (such as neem oil or white oil). For severe infestations, repeat applications may be necessary. The discolouration won't reverse, but with proper treatment the new growth will be healthy.

Growing tips

Prune and propagate
If your happy plant hasn't been growing in optimal conditions, then it may end up fairly tall, leggy and sparse. The good news is that you can easily fix this by pruning it back, which will promote new growth. Move the plant to a warm, brightly lit spot out of direct sun, and water when the potting mix is nearly dry. Propagate the cut section by placing it into a glass vase with water or into a pot filled with propagating mix (a blend of one part general potting mix and one part perlite or washed river sand).

Tenderheart
OTTOLENGHI SIMPLE
JERUSALEM
SAMI TAMIMI

Lucky bamboo

Dracaena sanderiana

Care
Low maintenance

Pet friendly
No

Light
Medium to bright, indirect light

Despite its common name, the lucky bamboo isn't actually bamboo, nor is it part of the same family as bamboo, Poaceae. It earned the name from its bamboo-like appearance, which is highlighted by the distinctive markings along its stems.

A symbol of health and prosperity, the lucky bamboo is readily available at garden centres and florists because it's a popular gift during Lunar New Year. It's also an ideal house-warming present because it's thought to bring wealth and harmony to the home.

It's usually sold as rooted stem cuttings. They have been cut and sealed with green wax on one end, while the other end has been rooted in water and stabilised with small pebbles. You'll often find a single stem planted in a decorative pot, but there may be multiple stems bundled tightly together or woven into an ornamental arrangement. It's said that the more stems, the more luck, good health and fortune!

The cut stem of the lucky bamboo will not grow in height. Instead, new shoots emerge from the node at the end of the cutting, giving the plant a lush, leafy appearance. The shoots can grow quite tall, but you can always cut them back if they become too big for your space.

All the dirt on the lucky bamboo

Light
The lucky bamboo grows best in medium to bright, indirect light. It can tolerate low light, but its growth will slow and its leaves may yellow and drop.

Potting mix
Use a free-draining potting mix, such as a cacti and succulent mix. Alternatively, if you wish to grow only in water, then wash the roots thoroughly and place the cutting into a vase or container filled with water and pebbles or stones for stability.

Fertiliser
Feed with a diluted indoor plant fertiliser, using a much weaker concentration than recommended, when the plant is actively growing during spring and summer.

Water
Water when the potting mix is nearly dry. If the plant has been grown in water, then top up or change the water in the vase or container every few weeks. The lucky bamboo can be sensitive to chlorine, so leave tap water to sit overnight to allow the chlorine to evaporate before using the water on your plants. Distilled water and rainwater are both better options.

Humidity
The lucky bamboo isn't picky about humidity and thrives in the standard level of humidity found in most homes.

Common problems of the lucky bamboo

Yellowing leaves and stems

Symptom
Leaves turning yellow, often followed by stem yellowing.

Cause
There are a few reasons why this may be happening. They include overwatering (or poor drainage), underwatering, watering with tap water or excessive use of fertiliser.

Solution
To prevent issues with overwatering and root rot, ensure that the pot has adequate drainage holes and is filled with a free-draining potting mix made for cacti and succulents. Remove the plant from the pot, and assess the damage; cut away any mushy, foul-smelling roots. If the stem is yellowing, then prune back as much of the affected growth as possible until you reach healthy green tissue, then repot into fresh potting mix.

If the plant is underwatered, then the stems may appear wrinkled. To avoid this, water when the potting mix is nearly dry, and always use filtered water or tap water that has been left to sit overnight to allow the chlorine to evaporate.

The lucky bamboo does not need copious amounts of plant food. To keep it happy, feed it with a heavily diluted indoor plant fertiliser once a month in spring and summer.

Growing tips

Promote good vibes in the home
According to feng shui principles, the specific placement of lucky bamboo in your home can attract certain energies that affect aspects of your life. For example, locating it in your office encourages financial success, while positioning it on your dining-room table invites abundance. However, you should avoid keeping lucky bamboo in your bedroom because its energetic properties may disrupt the calm and restful environment needed for sleep. Whether or not you believe in feng shui, it can't hurt to try placing your lucky bamboo in a favourable location!

MILK & SUGAR
ClothBound
OCEAN POOLS
Brooklyn Interiors
The Museum of Modern Art, New York

Mother-in-law's tongue

Dracaena trifasciata (syn. *Sansevieria trifasciata*)

Care
Low maintenance

Pet friendly
No

Light
Low to bright, indirect light

Also known as sansevieria (it was initially placed in the *Sansevieria* genus before being reclassified as *Dracaena*), the mother-in-law's tongue has long, narrow, sword-shaped leaves with green patterning and yellow margins. It's low maintenance and famously hard to kill, so it's a must-have plant for beginners.

The mother-in-law's tongue is often shunned in the home because it's widely displayed in virtually every public forum, including shopping centres, office lobbies and waiting rooms. Its ubiquity can make it seem less than unique or exciting to plant enthusiasts, but there's so much to love about this species! Its resilience and ability to adapt to various environments make it a fantastic houseplant. Native to western Africa, it naturally thrives in diverse settings - from tropical forests to savannas - demonstrating its capacity to flourish under different conditions and care levels.

The mother-in-law's tongue is the most widely recognised member of a diverse *Dracaena* group collectively known as snake plants. This group contains a multitude of species and cultivars - such as cylindrical snake plant (*Dracaena angolensis*) and whale fin (*Dracaena masoniana*) - which offer unique sizes, shapes, colours and patterns, making them a delight to explore and collect.

Renowned for their striking, architectural forms, snake plants provide a bold contrast to softer greenery, so they're perfect for adding visual interest to a range of indoor spaces. They can be styled in many ways, from compact desk companions and accents on side tables or shelves to tall, floor-sized statement pieces. These plants are super easy to propagate, too. Simply take leaf cuttings or divide the plant.

All the dirt on the mother-in-law's tongue

Light
The mother-in-law's tongue is adaptable to a range of light levels. Indoors, it grows best in bright, indirect light, but it will also tolerate lower light conditions. While it won't thrive in low light, it will still survive and continue to add greenery to your space.

Potting mix
Use a potting mix made for cacti and succulents.

Fertiliser
Apply a controlled-release fertiliser at the beginning of spring, reapplying as directed.

Water
Water when the top 2.5-5 centimetres (1-2 inches) of potting mix is dry. The mother-in-law's tongue will tolerate long periods without water, but don't neglect it completely.

Humidity
The mother-in-law's tongue is not particularly fussy about humidity. It's adaptable and will tolerate a range of levels.

Choice species and cultivars of the mother-in-law's tongue

Cylindrical snake plant (*Dracaena angolensis*, syn. *Sansevieria cylindrica*)

An unusual species, it has fleshy, cylindrical, spear-like foliage arranged in a fan-like pattern. Many nurseries sell it with the leaves braided.

Whale fin (*Dracaena masoniana*, syn. *Sansevieria masoniana*)

This is one of my favourite snake plants, thanks to its broad, paddle-like leaves that resemble whale fins. Variegated forms are available, too.

***Dracaena pethera* var. *pulchra* 'Silver Blue' (syn. *Sansevieria kirkii* var. *pulchra* 'Silver Blue')**

This cultivar has broad, stout, leathery, blue-green leaves with wavy margins, pointed tips and green stripes. The leaves are arranged in a rosette. A cultivar of the same plant in bronze-coppery tones - 'Coppertone' - is also available.

***Dracaena trifasciata* 'Bantel's Sensation'**

An attractive, upright plant, it has long, narrow, sword-like leaves that are dark green with bold, white, vertical stripes.

Common problems of the mother-in-law's tongue

Leaves folding over

Symptom
Wrinkled, limp, floppy leaves.

Cause
Leaf drooping in snake plants can result from underwatering, overwatering or insufficient light. With underwatered plants, the potting mix will feel completely dry; for overwatered plants, the potting mix will feel consistently moist or soggy. If you've positioned your plant in a room with insufficient light, then conditions will be fairly dim throughout the day with no direct or filtered light reaching the plant.

Solution
While snake plants can tolerate dry periods, prolonged neglect can cause their leaves to lose structural integrity, and the leaves subsequently fold. Water plants when the top 2.5–5 centimetres (1–2 inches) of potting mix is dry. Leaves won't regain their upright habit, but you can stake them for support. Alternatively, remove the leaves, cut off the damaged parts, and use the rest for propagation.

Excess moisture can lead to root rot, which compromises the plant's ability to absorb water and nutrients. As a result, the leaves become soft, mushy and weak, causing them to droop and collapse. To address this, remove any rotting leaves by cutting them off at the base. If parts of the leaf are healthy, then cut those parts off and use them for propagation.

Before watering again, check the potting mix first. If the mix is moist, then leave watering for a few days. If the potting mix is completely saturated, then you may want to consider repotting your plant into fresh mix.

Extended periods of little to no light cause leaves to weaken. The leaves may become narrow and elongated as the plant tries to reach for any available light. Eventually, the leaves collapse. Move the plant to a location with better light conditions. If natural light is limited, then consider grow lights. Trim any weakened leaves to encourage new, healthier growth.

Yellowing leaves

Symptom
Yellowing, mushy leaves, and foliage may collapse or break at the base. There may be sunken, water-soaked, brown or yellow spots on the leaves.

Cause
Overwatering and/or poor drainage can lead to root rot. Snake plants need well-drained potting mix to thrive, so ensure that your pot has drainage holes, and use a suitable potting mix (such as a cacti and succulent mix) to prevent excess moisture. Always check the potting mix moisture level before watering.

Solution
Remove the plant from the pot, and assess the roots. Healthy roots are firm and white, while rotting roots will be brown or black and soft, and emit a foul odour. If the majority of the roots are affected, then it's best to discard the plant. However, if most of the roots are healthy, then prune the damaged roots, sterilising the secateurs between each cut to avoid spreading any pathogens, and repot the plant into fresh potting mix.

Bleached leaves

Symptom
Pale, washed-out appearance.

Cause
Exposure to direct sun.

Solution
Prolonged exposure to direct sun can cause the leaves to become pale and look washed out. Move the plant out of direct sun and into bright, indirect light. While affected leaves won't recover, new growth will have a normal colour.

Brown or white spots on leaves

Symptom
Brown or white, hard or soft spots on the leaves. Foliage may also feel sticky to the touch.

Cause
Scale (sap-sucking insects).

Solution
Treat with a horticultural oil, applying as directed. Repeat applications may be required for severe infestations. Even after treatment, dead scale can still persist on the plant, so wipe the leaves with a microfibre cloth or paper towel to remove any remaining pests.

Growing tips

Divide and repot your snake plant
Snake plants are slow growing, but over time they'll fill the pot; their underground rhizomes (root-like stems) will often send out new shoots through the drainage holes as they continue to spread. Once the pot becomes crowded, it's a good idea to move the plant into a larger pot. If you don't want a larger pot plant, then divide the clump and repot the pieces into smaller pots.

To divide and repot a snake plant, grab a clean, sharp pair of secateurs, then follow these step-by-step instructions:

1. Remove the clump from the pot, and tease out the roots.
2. Use secateurs to separate the plants, taking care to keep the roots intact.
3. Repot each division into a clean, new container with fresh cacti and succulent potting mix.
4. Water in well with a diluted seaweed solution – this helps to promote root growth and reduce transplant shock.
5. Position the new plants in a brightly lit spot, out of direct sun.

THE SILVER SPOON
neil perry good food
SALT
FAT
ACID
HEAT
Samin
Nosrat
COOKED
MICHAEL POLLAN
ON
FOOD
AND
THE
SCIENC
AND
THE
KITCHE
SHORTBREAD
aarke

Fern leaf cactus

Epiphyllum chrysocardium (syn. *Selenicereus chrysocardium*)

Care
Low maintenance

Pet friendly
Yes

Light
Bright, indirect light

This is such a beautiful plant, don't you think? The fern leaf cactus looks similar to the fishbone cactus, but its broader, lush, flattened stems (cladodes) give it a softer appearance. As it grows, it spills wildly out of the pot; this quality makes it fabulous for imparting a tropical feel to indoor spaces.

It's a jungle cactus that grows as an epiphyte in the crooks of trees in its native Mexico. Unlike its desert cousins, it thrives in lower light, making it an excellent houseplant. However, it won't handle prolonged dry conditions, so be sure not to neglect its watering needs.

The fern leaf cactus can produce large white or pale pink blooms, but they are rarely seen in an indoor setting. If you want to encourage this, then it's best to position the plant outside.

When keeping it indoors, place the fern leaf cactus on a shelf or hang it from the ceiling to add a sculptural element to your vertical space and so you can fully enjoy its free-flowing, luscious stems. If the full-sized plant is too big for your shelf space, then you can simply grow cuttings in decorative vases or recycled jars.

You can also mount a fern leaf cactus onto a board using sphagnum moss, but be aware that you'll need to water it more often because moss dries out more quickly than potting mix. It makes for an intriguing display, though!

All the dirt on the fern leaf cactus

Light
The fern leaf cactus thrives in bright, indirect light. A few hours of direct sun in the morning is ideal, but it should be filtered for the remainder of the day.

Potting mix
Use a moist, well-drained potting mix, such as two parts premium potting mix blended with one part perlite and one part orchid bark.

Fertiliser
Apply a general-purpose controlled-release fertiliser at the beginning of spring, reapplying as directed. Alternatively, once a month from spring to late summer, apply a liquid fertiliser that has been diluted to half strength.

Water
Water when the top 2.5–5 centimetres (1–2 inches) of potting mix is dry.

Humidity
The fern leaf cactus can tolerate the standard level of humidity found in most homes. It will appreciate a little more humidity if you can manage it, but it's not necessary. To maintain a stable environment, it's best to avoid placing the plant near draughts or air-conditioning vents.

Common problems of the fern leaf cactus

Surprisingly, this plant doesn't seem to be plagued with problems. Overwatering or incorrect potting mix may lead to issues with root rot, but provided you use a moist, well-drained potting mix and only water when it's nearly dry, then your plant will be pretty happy.

Growing tips

Propagate your fern leaf cactus
Whether your fern leaf cactus has grown too large and needs a haircut, or it's looking a little bald at the top, propagation is a simple and rewarding way to rejuvenate your plant or to expand your cacti collection.

Grab a sharp pair of secateurs, then follow these step-by-step instructions:

1. Take a 7–10-centimetre (2¾–4-inch) cutting from the end of a stem (cladode).
2. Allow the cutting to callous over by placing it in a cool, dry spot for a couple of days.
3. Fill a small pot or tray with a suitable potting mix (such as a cacti and succulent mix), and insert the cut end.
4. Water in well, then position the pot in a warm, brightly lit spot out of direct sun.
5. Allow the potting mix to nearly dry out between waterings. Roots should form within four to six weeks.

IT GRASSO
2012
DE PAUME

Devil's ivy

Epipremnum aureum

Care
Low maintenance

Pet friendly
No

Light
Bright, indirect light

Reliable, dependable and tough to kill – these words perfectly describe the devil's ivy. This plant is a must-have for beginners because it offers both ease of care and aesthetic appeal. As a trailing or scrambling vine, it will spill over the sides of pots or hanging baskets, climb up a totem or moss pole, or festoon walls that have hooks for support. Just be cautious with this last option, especially in rental homes, because the aerial roots can leave marks on walls.

The classic form has small to medium, heart-shaped leaves with green and yellow mottling. When grown in ideal conditions, the leaves can become quite large. In its native warm and humid environments, the plant uses its aerial roots to clamber up trees, producing mature foliage that is large and fenestrated. Interestingly, during the height of monstera's popularity, many enthusiasts mistakenly believed that they had found a variegated species of that genus when they had actually encountered a mature devil's ivy, which shares a similar growth habit and leaf shape.

The devil's ivy is an easy plant to propagate: simply cut off a piece of the vine and root it in water. Many people choose to leave it in water as it grows, enjoying the simplicity of maintenance. Pair the cutting with elegant glassware for a beautiful statement, or opt for an eclectic display using a mix of recycled jars in various shapes and sizes.

All the dirt on the devil's ivy

Light
The devil's ivy thrives in bright, indirect light but is tolerant of medium to low light. If the light is low, then the plant may lose its variegation, growth will slow, and new leaves may emerge smaller than normal.

Potting mix
Use a premium potting mix. You can add perlite to assist with drainage and to help maintain the integrity of the mix, if desired. Blend five parts premium potting mix with one part perlite.

Fertiliser
Liquid feed regularly during the warmer months, or apply a controlled-release fertiliser at the beginning of spring, reapplying as directed.

Water
Water when the top 2.5–5 centimetres (1–2 inches) of potting mix is dry. Once established, the devil's ivy can tolerate slightly longer periods between watering, but be careful not to let it go too long. If underwatered, the leaves and stems will begin to wilt.

Humidity
The devil's ivy is adaptable to the standard level of humidity found in most homes. While it prefers medium humidity, it can tolerate lower levels. However, if it's placed near windows or air-conditioning vents, the leaves may dry out more quickly. So, monitor the plant, and move it to area away from direct draughts if necessary.

Choice cultivars of the devil's ivy

Epipremnum aureum
'Goldilocks'

All of the leaves on this cultivar are vibrant yellow to neon green, making it a standout among its green counterparts.

Epipremnum aureum
'Manjula'

I love the variegation on this cultivar. The rounded, heart-shaped, green leaves are beautifully accented with white and cream swirls. As it's heavily variegated, it's best to give this specimen a spot in bright, indirect light - otherwise the variegation may become less pronounced.

Epipremnum aureum
'Marble Queen'

As the name suggests, this cultivar features stunning green and white marbling on its narrow, heart-shaped leaves. The foliage can range from mostly creamy white with green speckles to mainly green with touches of creamy white.

Common problems of the devil's ivy

Leafless stems

Symptom
Sections of the vines are leafless.

Cause
Insufficient light is often the culprit. This issue typically arises when the devil's ivy is grown in a way that limits the access of light to certain parts of the vines, such as when it sprawls across a wall. After an extended period of inadequate light, the leaves may drop, leaving sections of the vines bare.

Solution
While new shoots may eventually form on these bare vines, it's more effective to cut back the plant to the bushiest part. This encourages new growth and revitalises the plant. Additionally, consider repositioning the plant to ensure that it has consistent access to light for healthier development.

Growing tips

Train your devil's ivy
Training your devil's ivy to climb can add vertical interest to your space while encouraging larger and more dramatic foliage.

Grab a support of your choice (moss or coir pole, recycled fence paling or wire trellis) and some soft garden ties, then follow these step-by-step instructions:

1. Insert the support into the pot, and push it down to stabilise it.
2. Guide the vines towards the support, and secure them with the soft garden ties. Avoid tying too tightly because this can damage the vines.
3. Aerial roots will eventually form and latch on to the support.
4. If you're using a moss or coir pole, then regularly moisten the surface to encourage roots to grip. For other supports, regularly guide the vines to ensure that the plant continues climbing.

YAMAHA

Rubber plant

Ficus elastica

Care
Low maintenance

Pet friendly
No

Light
Bright, indirect light

If there was one plant you could depend on for both good looks and low maintenance, then it would have to be the rubber plant. This species has large, leathery, glossy, dark green leaves that exude elegance. It's robust, too, tolerating a range of conditions, and its various cultivars offer a range of diverse variegation and colour to bring life to your home.

As it matures, it will grow into a large tree with a single trunk or multiple stems, making it a versatile choice if you're after a bold statement plant. Its impressive size allows it to stand alone as a striking floor feature, but it also pairs beautifully with plants of varying textures, colours and growth habits to create a vibrant, jungle-like scene. The leaves tend to get dusty and can be marked by water spots; simply wipe them clean with a moistened microfibre cloth or, for extra shine, use a horticultural oil (such as neem oil).

While it's low maintenance, the rubber plant still appreciates some attention. Rotate it occasionally to ensure even growth and light exposure. Handle with care, though - snapping a leaf or pruning a branch releases a milky white sap that can irritate the skin and is toxic if ingested.

This is a stunning indoor plant, but think twice before planting it outside in the garden. It can reach a towering height of 30 metres (100 feet) or more and develop numerous aerial roots for support as it grows. While it certainly looks amazing, it's definitely not a tree you want in your backyard!

All the dirt on the rubber plant

Light
The rubber plant thrives in bright, indirect light. If it's placed in low-light situations, then the leaves will begin to drop. Consider a grow light if you don't have sufficient light in your space.

Potting mix
Use a well-drained premium potting mix. You can add perlite to assist with drainage and to help maintain the integrity of the mix, if desired. Blend two parts premium potting mix with one part perlite.

Fertiliser
Liquid feed regularly during the warmer months, or apply a controlled-release fertiliser at the beginning of spring, reapplying as directed.

Water
Water when the top 2.5-5 centimetres (1-2 inches) of potting mix is dry. Ensure that the water runs through the drainage holes at the bottom of the pot.

Humidity
The rubber plant is adaptable to the standard level of humidity found in most homes. However, it prefers a higher level of humidity if you can manage it. For ways to boost indoor humidity, see page 26.

Choice cultivars of the rubber plant

Ficus elastica
'Burgundy'

Boasting shiny, deep green to near-black foliage with distinctive new growth that is pink, this cultivar is an attractive addition to any space. It looks particularly striking when it fills out the pot as a multi-stemmed plant, offering a beautiful contrast to surrounding plants.

Ficus elastica
'Tineke'

Sporting creamy, variegated leaves accented by soft shades of green and pink, this is a true statement piece. Be sure to provide plenty of bright, indirect light to help maintain the variegation and vibrant colours. *Ficus elastica* 'Shivereana' is another stunning variegated cultivar.

Growing tips

Fix a leggy plant
If your rubber plant has grown leggy and bare because of low-light conditions, overwatering or other factors, then a simple prune can help to rejuvenate it. Use a sharp pair of secateurs to cut back the plant to its bushiest point. Ensure that there is at least 15 centimetres (6 inches) of stem above the potting mix. Continue caring for the plant as usual, checking the moisture of the potting mix before watering, and you should notice new growth within six to eight weeks. It's best to do this during the warmer months, when the plant is actively growing.

Don't discard the cut section. Propagate it by dipping the cut end in a rooting hormone and planting it in a pot filled with a propagating mix (a blend of one part general potting mix and one part perlite or washed river sand). Position in a warm, brightly lit spot out of direct sun, and water regularly to keep the mix evenly moist. You can also place a plastic bag or cloche over the top to help maintain a warm, humid environment, which encourages root development. Remove the cover periodically for airflow, otherwise your plant may develop root rot.

Common problems of the rubber plant

Falling leaves

Symptom
Dropping of lower leaves. They may be curled and droopy before falling.

Cause
Insufficient light and/or overwatering.

Solution
The rubber plant needs bright, indirect light. If the light is too low, then the plant may start to shed its lower leaves. Move it to a spot where it can receive more light, but avoid direct sun, which can scorch the leaves.

Excessive watering can cause the roots to become waterlogged, leading to leaf drop. Ensure that the potting mix is well-drained, and allow the top 2.5–5 centimetres (1–2 inches) of potting mix to dry out before watering again.

White, cottony fluff

Symptom
White, cotton-like fluff on leaves and stems, often accompanied by a sticky residue.

Cause
Mealybugs (sap-sucking insects). The sticky residue is honeydew, a by-product of mealybugs.

Solution
Treat the plant with an insecticidal soap, horticultural oil or suitable pesticide. Since these treatments work on contact, thoroughly spray both the pests and the affected parts of the plant. Repeat as necessary, and isolate the plant to prevent the infestation from spreading.

Silvery leaves

Symptom
Leaves have a silvery, mottled appearance on the surface. Fine webbing may be observed between the leaves and stems.

Cause
Spider mites (sap-sucking arachnids).

Solution
Remove the worst-affected leaves, and treat the plant with an insecticidal soap, horticultural oil (such as neem oil or white oil) or suitable miticide (such as products containing abamectin). Always follow the label instructions carefully.

Saturday Night Pasta
The Essentials of Classic Italian Cooking
Marcella Hazan
EAT NYC
Saturday Night Pasta
NEIGHBOURHOOD
FAMILY
Home
GREEN THUMB
MAPS

Fiddle leaf fig

Ficus lyrata

Care
Medium maintenance

Pet friendly
No

Light
Bright, indirect light

The fiddle leaf fig first captured the hearts of thousands - probably millions - of people over a decade ago. It may even have been the plant that ignited the green revolution in home decor, sparking a new appreciation for bringing nature indoors.

With its strikingly large, textured, glossy green leaves and impressive stature, it's easy to see why the fiddle leaf fig is popular among interior designers and plant fanatics. Plus, it photographs well - need I say more?

But as popular as the fiddle leaf fig is, many people struggle to keep it alive. They tend to position it in the most aesthetically pleasing spot, rather than in the optimal position for growth, and soon its leaves begin to droop - and eventually drop - leaving behind a bare stem and a sad pot of potting mix. So, they try again with a new fiddle leaf fig: placing it in a different spot, watering it more (or less), praying to the plant gods ... but ultimately it meets the same fate.

The most important thing to understand about the fiddle leaf fig is how it grows in its native environment, so you can create similar conditions in your home. It's native to western Africa, where it grows in moist, lowland rainforests. Here, it becomes a large tree, up to 20 metres (65 feet) tall, and it spends most of its life in bright, indirect light (shaded by the canopy above) and in medium to high levels of humidity (>80 per cent). While this makes it sound like you can only grow the fiddle leaf fig in a glasshouse, the plant is actually surprisingly adaptable to the home environment.

All the dirt on the fiddle leaf fig

Light
The fiddle leaf fig grows best in bright, indirect light or filtered light. It appreciates a few hours of direct sun in the morning, with bright surroundings for the remainder of the day. It's not tolerant of low light and will lose its leaves if it doesn't get enough of the right kind of light.

Potting mix
Blend two parts premium potting mix with one part perlite to assist with drainage.

Fertiliser
Liquid feed regularly during the warmer months, or apply a controlled-release fertiliser at the beginning of spring, reapplying as directed.

Water
Water when the top 2.5-5 centimetres (1-2 inches) of potting mix is dry. Ensure that the water runs through the drainage holes at the bottom of the pot. The leaves will start to drop if the potting mix becomes too dry.

Humidity
The fiddle leaf fig is generally happy with the standard level of humidity found in most homes. However, if it's kept near a window, doorway or climate-control devices (such as fans or heaters), the humidity will be lower than it prefers. Browning on the edges of leaves and constantly drooping foliage are signs that the humidity is too low, or the potting mix is drying out too quickly (in other words, you're not watering the plant as often as you should!). For ways to boost indoor humidity, see page 26.

Choice cultivars of the fiddle leaf fig

Ficus lyrata
'Bambino'

This cute plant is the miniature version of the fiddle leaf fig. The leaves are smaller, and it will only grow to about 1 metre (3 feet) tall. An ideal choice if you want the look of the fiddle leaf fig without the size.

Ficus lyrata
'Variegata'

Highly decorative and a great statement piece, this is the variegated version of the classic fiddle leaf fig. It can be hard to find and therefore comes with a hefty price tag, but goodness it's beautiful. It requires the same growing conditions as its green counterpart.

Growing tips

Encourage leaf growth
If your fiddle leaf fig has been reduced to a few leaves, then you can try 'notching' to encourage new growth on the bare stem. It's important that you have remedied the cause of the leaf loss before attempting this, as there is little point to encouraging growth on an unhealthy plant.

Grab a clean, sharp pair of secateurs or a blade, then follow these step-by-step instructions:

1. Look for a node (the bump along the stem where a leaf previously emerged or grew).
2. Use the secateurs or blade to make a shallow notch above the node. The notch should be about 1–1.5 centimetres ($^1/_3$–$^2/_3$ inches) deep and extend horizontally across the stem.
3. Provide regular ongoing care – including water, sunlight and fertiliser – to promote and support healthy growth.

Get the fiddle leaf fig to branch
A fiddle leaf fig tends to grow upwards, with one main stem. If you prune this stem, then this will promote branching and a bushier appearance. Identify the point on the stem from where you want new branches to emerge. Using a clean, sharp pair of secateurs, make a 45-degree-angle cut just above the closest node to remove the stem. This will prompt the plant to redirect its growth hormones to lateral (side) buds, stimulating the development of new branches.

Common problems of the fiddle leaf fig

Dull-looking leaves

Symptom
Leaves have a silvery sheen and lack the typical vibrant green hue. Fine webbing may be observed between the leaves and stems.

Cause
Spider mites (sap-sucking arachnids).

Solution
Treat with an insecticidal soap or suitable pesticide. Check the label for instructions, and use only as directed. Repeat treatments may be required. Damage to affected leaves is irreversible, but new growth will be unaffected if the spider mites have been eradicated.

Red/brown spots on leaves

Symptom
Small, dark red to brown spots appear on new leaves.

Cause
Moisture stress from irregular watering, especially during periods of growth. When the plant finally receives water, the roots absorb it faster than the plant can transpire or consume, leading to increased water pressure within the leaf cells. These cells burst, appearing as reddish brown spots on the leaves.

Solution
Remember to water when the top 2.5–5 centimetres (1–2 inches) of potting mix is dry. With good care, the spots will eventually disappear.

Loss of leaves

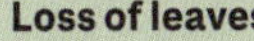

Symptom
Leaves are slowly or rapidly falling, leaving a mostly bare stem.

Cause
Plant is stressed due to poor lighting, poor drainage, a watering issue, or a pest/disease problem.

Solution
Follow the flow chart on page 45 to identify the specific cause and relevant solution.

Creeping fig

Ficus pumila

Care
Low maintenance

Pet friendly
No

Light
Bright, indirect light

I love the creeping fig. When grown outdoors, it clings to walls and other hard surfaces, vigorously covering them with its adventitious roots and crinkled, heart-shaped leaves. It adds a rustic charm to any outdoor area, creating the impression that nature is gently reclaiming the space.

As an indoor plant, the creeping fig is highly ornamental – just don't let it climb your walls! While it won't cause structural damage, it can remove paint and leave marks behind, making it a risky choice for renters. Instead, it's best appreciated by letting it trail over the side of a pot or hanging basket. You can also train it on a topiary trellis or other support. When small, it's ideal for tables, desks and shelves. But as it grows, especially if it's supported by a trellis, it's better to place it on the floor. It also thrives in terrariums, where it can serve as a ground cover or be trained to climb a piece of driftwood or a rock.

In its native environment of tropical and subtropical forests across Asia, the creeping fig grows as a climbing vine, attaching itself to trees and rock faces. There, it thrives in warm, humid conditions and dappled light. However, it's adaptable and can grow in full sun to partial shade outdoors, although it prefers bright, indirect light when cultivated indoors.

As the creeping fig matures, its leaves become larger, thicker and more leathery, and the plant transforms into a woody climber. These mature leaves are vastly different from the juvenile forms and are generally considered to be less attractive. You're unlikely to see mature leaves indoors, though. If you do, then simply prune them off. Take care when pruning because the milky sap can irritate your skin.

All the dirt on the creeping fig

Light
The creeping fig thrives in bright, indirect light. In lower light levels, the leaves tend to drop.

Potting mix
Blend two parts premium potting mix with one part perlite to assist with drainage.

Fertiliser
Feed regularly with an indoor plant or general-purpose fertiliser in spring and summer.

Water
The creeping fig can be sensitive to both underwatering and overwatering, so only water when the potting mix is nearly dry. To test, insert your finger 2.5–5 centimetres (1–2 inches) into the mix, and feel if the mix is moist or dry. If the mix is moist, then leave watering for a few days; if it's dry, then give the plant a good drink.

Humidity
The creeping fig is adaptable to the standard level of humidity found in most homes, but it thrives in a higher level if you can manage it. To boost humidity, place the plant on a tray filled with pebbles and water, or group it with other plants. Be sure to keep it away from air-conditioning vents, heaters and cold draughts because these will dry out the air quickly.

Choice cultivars of the creeping fig

Ficus pumila
'Ice Caps'

This cultivar features leaves with white edges that contrast beautifully with the green centres. It's a nice change from the traditional all-green variety, especially if you're in the market for something that pops.

Ficus pumila
'Minima'

As the name suggests, this cultivar has small leaves, giving it a more delicate and compact appearance than the standard variety. Despite its petite size, it remains a vigorous grower. Prune it back to maintain its shape if necessary.

Common problems of the creeping fig

Dried, shrivelled leaves

Symptom
Leaves are dry, brittle and shrivelled, with a crispy texture. The plant may look limp or wilted overall.

Cause
Underwatering or low humidity.

Solution
If the plant has been underwatered, then give it a good soak and ensure that the water runs through the drainage holes at the bottom of the pot. Resume a more regular watering routine to prevent future issues. The dried leaves won't recover, so cut back the plant to where it's green or to ground level in order to promote new growth – hopefully it's not too far gone!

If humidity dips too low or there is a sudden increase in room temperature – especially on a hot summer day – this can dry out the plant, causing the leaves to shrivel and crisp. Maintain consistent humidity by keeping the plant away from draughts, air-conditioning vents and heating vents. Consider placing the plant on a tray filled with pebbles and water or using a humidifier to keep the air-moisture level steady. For other ways to boost indoor humidity, see page 26. If hot conditions are expected and the room gets fairly warm and stuffy, then I'd recommend moving your plant to a cooler area (such as the bathroom or laundry) to help keep it cool.

Growing tips

Train a creeping fig
The creeping fig loves to climb. While it's not essential to encourage this behaviour in your home, it can create a stunning, decorative feature. You can train the plant to wrap its stems around a wire trellis or adhere to a surface (such as a recycled fence paling or coir pole). Before you begin, the plant may need to be repotted into a larger container to accommodate your chosen support structure.

Insert the support structure into the pot. Gently twist the plant's stems around the support, and use soft garden ties or staples to secure them if necessary. As the plant grows, continue to guide the stems around the structure, and it will gradually find its own way upward.

Nerve plant

Fittonia albivenis

Care
Low to medium maintenance

Pet friendly
Yes

Light
Medium to bright, indirect light

This houseplant is on the smaller side, but it's by no means a shrinking violet. The nerve plant - also known as the mosaic plant - has small, green leaves with prominent, white veins, creating a striking colour contrast; some cultivars have pink or red veins. The veining is often so bold that the leaves appear vividly white, pink or red. While the foliage is typically smooth-edged, some cultivars are ruffled, adding to their charm.

Note that the form with white veins is technically classified as *Fittonia albivenis* ('albivenis' means white veins). Plants with red or pink veins, however, fall under *Fittonia albivenis* Verschaffeltii Group. You may come across the name *Fittonia verschaffeltii*, but this species doesn't exist; it's a synonym of *Fittonia albivenis* Verschaffeltii Group.

Native to the tropical rainforests of South America, the nerve plant flourishes on the forest floor, in humid and shaded conditions, making it an ideal indoor plant. Growing to just 15 centimetres (6 inches) tall, it's a perfect desk companion, accent on a side or coffee table, or member of a decorative plant display. It also shines as a terrarium specimen. I keep mine in a closed terrarium, which is the easiest way to maintain the plant - it provides humidity and it's self-watering.

Although the nerve plant remains short, it loves to spread, quickly filling out a pot and gently spilling over the edge. It's also easy to propagate: take cuttings or divide the plant to fill out the pot more quickly or to create new plants. If it gets too large or some stems become leggy from lack of light, then simply cut back the stems to encourage fuller growth.

With a wide array of cultivars to choose from, the biggest challenge is deciding which ones to buy - and how many to add to your collection!

All the dirt on the nerve plant

Light
The nerve plant grows best in medium to bright, indirect light. It can tolerate low light, but its colours may dull and the veins may become less pronounced. Avoid placing in direct sun because this will scorch the leaves.

Potting mix
Blend equal parts premium potting mix, perlite and coco peat.

Fertiliser
Dilute a liquid fertiliser to half strength, and apply once a month during the warmer months.

Water
Water when the top 2.5–5 centimetres (1–2 inches) of potting mix is dry.

Humidity
The nerve plant prefers a humidity level of 50 per cent or higher, so group it with other plants or sit it on top of a saucer filled with pebbles and water. Avoid placing it near air-conditioning vents or heaters because these will dry the air and cause humidity to drop. For other ways to boost indoor humidity, see page 26.

Choice species of the nerve plant

Giant-leaved nerve plant (*Fittonia gigantea*)

If you weren't satisfied with the petite species and its cultivars, then you'll be delighted to know that this species can grow 60–80 centimetres (24–32 inches) tall with leaves that are 16 centimetres (6¼ inches) long and 8–10 centimetres (3–4 inches) wide. The foliage is richly green with white or red-pink venation.

Common problems of the nerve plant

Leaves curling and shrivelling

Symptom
The plant appears wilted, with dry, curled leaves and limp stems.

Cause
Overwatering, underwatering or low humidity.

Solution
Wet or soggy potting mix deprives the roots of oxygen, causing them to rot. This can lead to droopy stems and shrivelled leaves because the roots are no longer able to take up moisture properly. Only water when the top 2.5–5 centimetres (1–2 inches) of potting mix is dry, and ensure that the plant is in a well-drained potting mix.

On the other hand, don't let the potting mix completely dry out between waterings. Check the mix, and water thoroughly when the top 2.5–5 centimetres (1–2 inches) of potting mix is dry.

The nerve plant loves humid environments, so if the humidity dips too low for too long, then the leaves can curl and shrivel. Increase humidity around the plant by grouping it with other plants or by planting it in a terrarium. For other ways to boost indoor humidity, see page 26.

Growing tips

Fix a leggy, sparse nerve plant
When grown in poor lighting, the nerve plant can become leggy, with elongated internodes (the spaces between the nodes) as it stretches out in search of more light. This results in a sparse, straggly appearance – often with small leaves – rather than its usual compact, bushy growth.

To fix this, cut the plant back to the bushiest point. If there is none, prune it back to at least one node. Position it in a brighter spot, and resume regular care. I wouldn't bother propagating the leggy growth that you've trimmed off. Instead, focus on nurturing your nerve plant back to health. Once the plant has recovered and is thriving, then you can take cuttings from its healthier sections for propagation.

Calatheas

Goeppertia spp.

Care
Low to high maintenance

Pet friendly
Yes

Light
Bright, indirect light

Calatheas are among the most delightful indoor plants to collect. With a diverse array of shapes, sizes, patterns, textures and colours, they offer something for every plant enthusiast. They range from low-maintenance options, such as the peacock plant (*Goeppertia makoyana*), to diva-like personalities, such as *Goeppertia lietzei* 'White Fusion', so be wary of which one you choose – especially for your first!

Most calatheas grow to a height of 30–60 centimetres (12–24 inches) – occasionally reaching up to 1 metre (3 feet) – making them ideal for various spaces in the home. Their versatility allows for a range of styling options, with compact varieties perfect for desks and smaller areas, while big specimens can add a dramatic touch to larger settings.

Originally part of the *Calathea* genus, many species have now been reclassified into the *Goeppertia* genus, but they're still commonly referred to as calatheas. They're also called 'peacock plants' because many of them have showy, dramatic leaves. Some calatheas tend to fold up their leaves at night, as if they were praying, and open them in the morning. This phenomenon, known as nyctinasty, earns them the moniker 'prayer plants'. It's a natural response to changes in light and temperature, and common in the Marantaceae family, to which calatheas belong.

Like most houseplants, calatheas are native to tropical rainforests of Central and South America, where they grow in dappled light and consistent humidity. Give them similar conditions, and watch them thrive.

All the dirt on calatheas

Light
Calatheas thrive in bright, indirect light, though some can tolerate medium light levels.

Potting mix
Use a moist, well-drained potting mix. I like to combine one part premium potting mix with one part coco peat and one part perlite.

Fertiliser
Liquid feed regularly during the warmer months, or apply a controlled-release fertiliser at the beginning of spring, reapplying as directed.

Water
Water when the top 2.5–5 centimetres (1–2 inches) of potting mix is dry. Ensure that the water runs through the drainage holes at the bottom of the pot. The leaves will curl if the potting mix becomes too dry, putting the plant under unnecessary stress.

Humidity
Most calatheas prefer around 60 per cent humidity. There are a few non-fussy species, such as the peacock plant (*Goeppertia makoyana*, syn. *Calathea makoyana*), which can tolerate less, but the majority like it humid. Avoid placing them in draughty areas or near climate-control devices (such as air-conditioning vents or heaters). Browning along the leaf edges generally indicates low humidity. It's not bad for the plant, but it can be unsightly. Plants such as *Goeppertia orbifolia* (syn. *Calathea orbifolia*) and *Goeppertia lietzei* 'White Fusion' (syn. *Calathea lietzei* 'White Fusion') love warmth and humidity, upwards of 80 per cent. For ways to boost indoor humidity, see page 26.

Choice species and cultivars of calatheas

Rattlesnake plant (*Goeppertia insignis*, syn. *Calathea lancifolia*)

This eye-catching plant boasts long, narrow leaves with wavy edges. Each leaf features a striking pattern on top and a rich purple underside - great for adding visual drama to your space.

***Goeppertia lietzei* 'White Fusion' (syn. *Calathea lietzei* 'White Fusion')**

This is a stunning calathea! The leaves display an artistic fusion of creamy white and lush green, creating a beautiful marbled effect. On the reverse, they feature a soft purple hue that adds a gorgeous colour contrast. It thrives in high humidity, so be sure to pamper it to keep it looking its best.

Peacock plant (*Goeppertia makoyana*, syn. *Calathea makoyana*)

This classic calathea has broad, oval leaves with a similar patterning to the rattlesnake plant (*Goeppertia insignis*). It's sometimes called cathedral windows because the dark green markings against the delicate veining mimic the artistry of stained-glass windows.

***Goeppertia orbifolia* (syn. *Calathea orbifolia*)**

I'm captivated by its large, round leaves, and the silvery patterning is particularly mesmerising. It can grow wide and bushy, adding lushness to your space. However, it does need high humidity, so be prepared to meet its demands - otherwise, it might decline quickly.

Common problems of calatheas

Brown leaf tips

Symptom
Browning at the tips of the leaves.

Cause
This typically indicates low humidity. Hot or cool draughts dry out the air surrounding the plant, which causes the leaves to lose moisture faster than the plant can replace it.

Solution
Position the plant away from open windows and doorways, or any other sources of draughts. Additionally, keep it clear of heating or cooling vents. To maintain consistent humidity, place a shallow tray of water near the plant. For other ways to boost indoor humidity, see page 26.

Silvery, mottled leaves

Symptom
Silvery, mottled leaves accompanied by a sickly appearance and a noticeable decrease in plant health and vigour.

Cause
Spider mites (sap-sucking arachnids).

Solution
Spider mites thrive in dry conditions, so increasing humidity around the plant can help to deter them. Remove affected leaves, and spray the entire plant with an insecticidal soap. Repeat sprays may be needed, especially with severe infestations.

Growing tips

Renew your calathea
Is your calathea looking worse for wear or seemingly beyond saving? It happens – whether from neglect or a severe pest infestation. Fortunately, most calatheas are resilient and can often bounce back. Start by giving your plant a hard prune, trimming away most of the dead growth close to ground level. Water it well, then let it be. With a bit of patience, you might soon spot new growth emerging. I've often seen people relegate their 'dead' or struggling plant to a dingy corner outdoors, only to be pleasantly surprised that it grew back – so don't give up!

Umbrella trees

Heptapleurum spp.

Care
Low maintenance

Pet friendly
No

Light
Bright, indirect light

For those of you wanting a tree to liven up your indoors, the umbrella tree could be the answer! There are a handful of species that are perfect as houseplants, each showcasing the signature umbrella-like foliage that gives the genus its common name.

Umbrella trees are hardy, low-maintenance plants that grow into lush, bushy specimens with little effort - the Australian umbrella tree (*Heptapleurum actinophyllum*) is considered a weed in some areas, giving you an idea of how well it flourishes with little to no care. Bigger species work well as feature plants in large pots on the floor with other plants, while smaller, more compact species will sit perfectly alone on shelves or tabletops. Some are sold with a single trunk for a more tree-like appearance, while others have multiple trunks, giving them a fuller, shrub-like form.

The dwarf umbrella tree (*Heptapleurum arboricola*) is often sold with its roots exposed and anchored to a rock, mimicking the way some epiphytic plants grow with minimal potting mix. While it's not a true epiphyte, it can adapt to and thrive in this type of creative display. It makes an excellent bonsai specimen, too.

All the dirt on umbrella trees

Light
Umbrella trees thrive in bright, indirect light. If they're placed in low-light situations, then their leaves will yellow and drop.

Potting mix
Use a premium potting mix. You can also mix your own by combining equal parts premium potting mix, perlite, coco peat and orchid bark.

Fertiliser
Liquid feed regularly during the warmer months, or apply a controlled-release fertiliser at the beginning of spring, reapplying as directed.

Water
Water when the top 2.5–5 centimetres (1–2 inches) of potting mix is dry. Ensure that the water runs through the drainage holes at the bottom of the pot.

Humidity
Umbrella trees are adaptable to the standard level of humidity found in most homes. To maintain a stable environment, it's best to avoid placing the plants near heaters or air-conditioning vents.

Choice species of umbrella trees

Australian umbrella tree (*Heptapleurum actinophyllum*, syn. *Schefflera actinophylla*)

An Australian native, it has glossy, green, lance-shaped leaves radiating out from a single point. Given the right conditions indoors, it can grow 2 metres (7 feet) or more in height. It's considered a weed in some Australian states, as well as in other parts of the world. *Heptapleurum actinophyllum* 'Amate' is an improved form with large, glossy leaves, as well as better pest resistance and overall hardiness; *Heptapleurum actinophyllum* 'Amate Soleil' has the same features, but with vibrant chartreuse-coloured foliage.

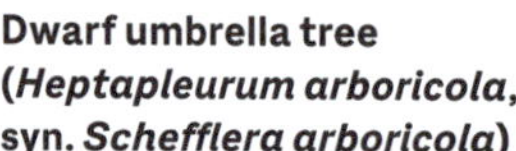

Dwarf umbrella tree (*Heptapleurum arboricola*, syn. *Schefflera arboricola*)

This species is much smaller than the Australian umbrella tree, typically reaching 1–1.5 metres (3–5 feet) in height – although it can be kept smaller with pruning. The leaves are bright green, but you can also find variegated creamy white or yellow versions.

***Heptapleurum schizophyllum* (syn. *Schefflera schizophyllum*)**

This species may not be a commonly grown houseplant yet, but it certainly deserves more attention. I have one in my collection, and I love its deeply lobed leaves. These set it apart from the simple, unlobed leaves of other umbrella trees.

Common problems of umbrella trees

Silvery leaves

Symptom
Leaves have a silvery, mottled appearance. Fine webbing may be observed between the leaves and stems.

Cause
Spider mites (sap-sucking arachnids).

Solution
Remove the worst-affected leaves, and treat the plant with an insecticidal soap, horticultural oil (such as neem oil or white oil) or suitable miticide (such as products containing abamectin). Always follow the label instructions.

Lumps and bumps on leaves

Symptom
Brown, white, black or coloured bumps on leaves and stems. They can be easily scratched off with your fingernail. The affected plant parts may also be covered in a sticky residue.

Cause
Scale (sap-sucking insects).

Solution
Treat with a horticultural oil because it coats their waxy shells and suffocates them. Alternatively, look for a systemic insecticide that targets sap-sucking insects, or carefully dab a cotton bud soaked in rubbing alcohol directly onto the pests.

White, cottony fluff

Symptom
White, cotton-like fluff on leaves and stems, often accompanied by a sticky residue.

Cause
Mealybugs (sap-sucking insects). The sticky residue is honeydew, a by-product of mealybugs.

Solution
Treat the plant with an insecticidal soap, horticultural oil or a suitable pesticide. Since these treatments work on contact, thoroughly spray both the pests and the affected parts of the plant. Repeat as necessary, and isolate the plant to prevent the infestation from spreading.

Growing tips

Fix a leggy umbrella tree
If your umbrella tree has become leggy – tall and thin with few leaves along the lower stem – then you can encourage fuller growth with some strategic pruning. Use a sharp pair of secateurs to 'top off' the plant (remove the crown), ensuring that the remaining stem is at least 15 centimetres (6 inches) high. While this may seem drastic, your plant will recover and grow back bushier.

Make the most of the crown by dipping the cut end in a rooting hormone and planting it in a pot filled with a propagating mix (a blend of one part general potting mix and one part perlite or washed river sand). Water regularly to keep the potting mix moist, and keep the plant in a warm, brightly lit spot out of direct sun. Roots usually start to appear in six to eight weeks.

Homalomenas

Homalomena spp.

Care
Low maintenance

Pet friendly
No

Light
Bright, indirect light

With their lush, glossy, heart- or spade-shaped leaves, homalomenas will inject vibrant tropical vibes into any space.

The genus *Homalomena* is part of the Araceae family, most of which make fabulous houseplants. Some forms are compact, while others grow into bushy plants up to 60 centimetres (24 inches) tall. You'll find a homalomena that's ideal for any space, from desks and tables to shelves and plant stands.

Native to various tropical regions of South America and southern Asia, homalomenas prefer warm, humid conditions and thrive in dappled light on the forest floor. While they're adaptable to most home environments, some of their leaves may turn yellow or drop if the temperature becomes too cold. To protect your plant during the colder months, insulate your pot with bubble wrap - especially if your home gets chilly in winter. This basic but effective solution will help to maintain warmth around the roots. (Incidentally, covering windows with bubble wrap is a great way to cheaply insulate your home - I learned that this past winter!)

Homalomenas steadily push out new growth, but they aren't super-fast growers, so there's no need to repot annually. They'll outgrow their pots eventually, at which point you can divide the plants and repot them, or simply move them to a larger container.

In recent years, some species of *Homalomena* have been reclassified as *Adelonema*, but many plant enthusiasts still refer to them by their original name - myself included. Ultimately, the name doesn't matter as much as the joy that these plants bring to your space.

All the dirt on homalomenas

Light
Homalomenas thrive in bright, indirect light. They can tolerate slightly lower light conditions, although growth may slow down. Keep the plants out of direct sun because it can scorch the leaves.

Potting mix
Use equal parts premium potting mix, perlite, coco peat and orchid bark.

Fertiliser
Liquid feed regularly during the warmer months, or apply a controlled-release fertiliser at the beginning of spring, reapplying as directed.

Water
Water when the top 2.5-5 centimetres (1-2 inches) of potting mix is dry.

Humidity
Homalomenas are adaptable to the standard level of humidity found in most homes. However, they prefer a higher level of humidity if you can manage it. Keep them away from heaters and air conditioners, and group them with other plants or sit them on a saucer filled with water and pebbles. For other ways to boost indoor humidity, see page 26.

Choice species and cultivars of homalomenas

***Adelonema wallisii* 'Camouflage' (syn. *Homalomena wallisii* 'Camouflage')**

It's easy to see how this cultivar earned its name. The foliage features a striking camouflage-like pattern, making it an intriguing and eye-catching piece of greenery. It's perfect for adding contrast and a point of difference to your collection.

***Homalomena rubescens* 'Maggie'**

A gorgeous cultivar, it has deeply veined, heart-shaped leaves and contrasting red stems. There's a variegated form, too (pictured below right), but it's difficult to find and often comes with a hefty price tag.

Common problems of homalomenas

Yellowing, dropping leaves

Symptom
Leaves are yellowing and falling off.

Cause
Overwatering and/or poor drainage, or prolonged exposure to cold temperatures.

Solution
Ensure that the pot has adequate drainage holes, and use a well-drained potting mix to prevent water pooling at the roots. Only water when the top 2.5–5 centimetres (1–2 inches) of potting mix is dry. Check by inserting your finger into the top of the mix. If it feels moist, then leave watering; if feels dry, then give the plant a good drink.

Homalomenas can be quite moody when the temperature drops below 15 degrees Celsius (59 degrees Fahrenheit). If you're not comfortable, then neither are they! To help your plant endure the cold weather, cover the pot in bubble wrap to provide insulation. If the look isn't to your taste, then simply slip the pot into a decorative cache pot (cover pot) to hide the bubble wrap and maintain your style while keeping your plant cosy.

Curled, droopy leaves

Symptom
Leaves are curling and drooping.

Cause
Underwatering.

Solution
When homalomenas are not getting enough water, their leaves may curl and droop as a sign of stress. Water when the top 2.5–5 centimetres (1–2 inches) of potting mix is dry, ensuring that the water runs through the drainage holes at the bottom of the pot.

Growing tips

Divide and propagate your homalomenas
As they mature, homalomenas naturally produce offshoots (smaller clumps of new plants) next to the parent plant. These offshoots make the plants fuller, but if the plants grow too large, then you can divide them to keep their size manageable.

Remove the plant from its pot, and tickle the potting mix to reveal the roots. If it's compacted, then you may need to use a dibbler, chopstick or something similar to loosen the potting mix. Have a close look at the base of the stems: you can typically make out the clumps of plants. Before dividing, ensure that each clump has healthy stems, leaves and roots. Use your hands to carefully pull the clumps apart. A sharp knife or pair of secateurs may help.

Place each clump into its own pot with fresh potting mix, making sure that the base of the plant is positioned at the same depth as before. Water the new plants thoroughly with a diluted seaweed solution, which encourages root growth and reduces transplant shock. Place the pots in a warm area with bright, indirect light to allow the new plants to settle.

Kentia palm

Howea forsteriana

Care
Low maintenance

Pet friendly
Yes

Light
Bright, indirect light

Palms have a way of bringing the tropics indoors. Their large, gracefully arching, deep green fronds create a calming, elegant atmosphere that instantly elevates any space. In my humble opinion, the Kentia palm is one of the best choices for the home. It's highly adaptable - tolerating low light and dry spells - making it perfect for those who occasionally neglect their plants. It's also slow growing, which means less time spent repotting. Resilient and forgiving, it's an excellent companion if you have a relaxed approach to plant care.

Thanks to its impressive size, the fully grown Kentia palm works best as a floor specimen, standing tall by the front door or adding a tropical touch to dining or living areas. Its tolerant nature also makes it a popular choice for offices.

The Kentia palm can start to look tattered if it's neglected for too long, but don't worry - it's a tough plant. As soon as you improve its growing conditions, new growth will emerge. You can then prune the old, damaged fronds and restore the palm's fresh appearance.

A special aspect of this plant is its origin: it's native to Lord Howe Island, a UNESCO World Heritage site known for its incredible natural beauty and biodiversity. By adding a Kentia palm to your space, you're bringing a piece of this unique landscape into your home. Cool, right?

All the dirt on the Kentia palm

Light
The Kentia palm grows best in bright, indirect light. It tolerates lower light conditions, but this will result in slower growth.

Potting mix
Combine three parts premium potting mix with one part perlite and one part orchid bark.

Fertiliser
Apply a controlled-release fertiliser in spring and summer. An organic, slow-release fertiliser works well, too. Look for one that is odourless or has a reduced odour if you find the smell offensive.

Water
Water when the top 2.5–5 centimetres (1–2 inches) of potting mix is dry. Ensure that the water runs through the drainage holes at the bottom of the pot.

Humidity
The Kentia palm is adaptable to the standard level of humidity found in most homes. While it thrives in an environment that's moist and warm, it's quite forgiving if those conditions aren't perfectly met.

Common problems of the Kentia palm

White, cottony fluff on leaves and stems

Symptom
White, fluffy clusters on leaves and stems. Affected plant parts may be covered in a sticky residue.

Cause
Mealybugs (sap-sucking insects). The sticky residue is honeydew, a by-product of mealybugs.

Solution
Treat the leaves and stems with an insecticidal soap or suitable pesticide.

Dots or bumps on leaves or stems

Symptom
Small, brown, white or coloured bumps on leaves or stems. They can be easily scratched off with your fingernail.

Cause
Scale (sap-sucking insects).

Solution
The common treatment for scale is horticultural oil, such as white oil. However, palms can be sensitive to oils, which may burn their leaves. Test on a small, inconspicuous area first; if no negative reaction (such as foliage burn or browning) occurs after a few days, then proceed with a more widespread application. Alternatively, consider using a systemic product, or carefully dab a cotton bud soaked in rubbing alcohol directly onto the pests.

Silvery, mottled foliage

Symptom
Silvering of leaf surfaces; webbing may be present.

Cause
Spider mites (sap-sucking arachnids).

Solution
Spray fronds with an insecticidal soap or a suitable miticide. Horticultural oil is also effective, but palms are often sensitive to oils – so, proceed with caution.

Browning fronds

Symptom
Fronds are turning brown at the tips or edges, progressing inwards.

Cause
Underwatering, overwatering, low humidity, exposure to direct sun or natural deterioration of older leaves.

Solution
If you have underwatered the plant, then the potting mix will feel completely dry to the touch. There may even be a gap between the potting mix and pot because the lack of moisture has made the potting mix shrink. Underwatering can cause leaves to become dry and brown. Leaves may also be droopy. When watering, ensure that the water runs through the drainage holes at the bottom of the pot. Then you'll know that you've given the plant a good drink. To fix an underwatered plant, water the plant well and see if it recovers after a few days. If not, then you may need to completely submerge the pot in a bucket of water to rehydrate the potting mix.

If you have overwatered the plant, then the potting mix will feel overly wet to the touch. Too much water can lead to root rot, which can cause leaves to yellow, brown and die. Always check the potting mix first before watering to see if the plant needs a drink. Insert your finger into the top 2.5–5 centimetres (1–2 inches) of potting mix. If the mix is moist, then leave watering; if it's dry, then give it a deep watering. To fix an overwatered plant, remove the dead or dying fronds and allow the potting mix to become nearly dry. If the potting mix is still soaking wet after a few days, then you may want to repot into fresh mix to give your plant the best chance of survival.

Is your plant sitting in front of or near an air conditioner or heater? Constant exposure to air from these units can lower the humidity in a home and cause Kentia palm fronds to dry out and brown on the edges. Move the palm away from air-conditioning vents, and increase humidity by grouping it with other plants or sitting it on a tray filled with pebbles and water. For other ways to boost indoor humidity, see page 26.

If the Kentia palm is positioned close to a window, then it may be exposed to direct sun. This often leads to dark brown or nearly black marks on the leaves, typically appearing in a random pattern on the side facing the window. To prevent this, move the plant further from the window or install a sheer curtain to filter the light.

If you're only seeing a few of the lower, older fronds brown and die, then this may simply be part of the plant's natural life cycle – older fronds naturally turn yellow and brown before dying. Simply trim away the dead fronds to keep the plant looking tidy.

Growing tips

Repot your Kentia palm
The Kentia palm can be sensitive to repotting, and will take some time to adjust after being transplanted. Fortunately, there is no need to do this often. The best time to repot is when the plant has outgrown its current pot – you may see roots poking out through the drainage holes, or there is not much give when you squeeze the plastic pot.

To minimise stress and transplant shock, avoid disturbing the roots when repotting, unless you need to cut away dead or circling roots. Water in well with a diluted seaweed solution to help reduce transplant shock and promote root growth.

Wax flowers

Hoya spp.

Care
Low to medium maintenance

Pet friendly
Yes

Light
Bright, indirect light

Wax flowers provide the best of both worlds: fabulous, interesting foliage and wonderfully perfumed blooms. Personally, it's the foliage that I find most captivating, but the clusters of waxy, star-shaped flowers are always a delightful bonus.

There are hundreds of wax flower species and cultivars, each with a unique leaf form. Some have gnarly, twisted leaves, others have heart-shaped leaves with splashes of white, and some even have large, round leaves like dinner plates.

Many wax flowers are epiphytic, vining plants with long, flexible stems that can either climb supports or trail gracefully over the sides of pots. They can be trained to grow around hoops or decorative trellises, creating an elegant display. Other species are considered 'basket types' because they don't twine, and they're best showcased in hanging pots or baskets.

One great aspect of wax flowers is that they enjoy being root-bound. This means that you can keep them in the same pot for several years before needing to repot. You can also mount them onto wooden boards for a decorative display. Ensure that the board is marine grade if you want it to last, or coat it with a waterproof sealant to protect it from moisture. However, mounted plants will require more frequent watering than those in pots because they dry out more quickly.

All the dirt on wax flowers

Light
Wax flowers prefer a position in bright, indirect light. A few hours of sun in the morning is ideal, with bright surroundings for the remainder of the day. They can tolerate slightly lower light levels, but they won't flower; new leaves will be smaller.

Potting mix
Use a moist, well-drained potting mix, such as fine orchid bark, or a blend of two parts premium potting mix, one part perlite and one part orchid bark. Wax flowers enjoy being snug in their pot, so frequent repotting isn't necessary. After a couple of years, give the plastic pot a squeeze; if there's not much give, then move the plant up to the next pot size to avoid overpotting, which can lead to water-retention issues. If your plant is in a hard pot, then check for roots emerging from the drainage holes and repot if necessary.

Fertiliser
Apply a controlled-release fertiliser during spring and summer. Alternatively, use a liquid fertiliser that has been diluted to half strength, applying it regularly during the warmer months.

Water
Water when the potting mix is nearly dry.

Humidity
Wax flowers have varying preferences when it comes to humidity. Some, such as the porcelain flower (*Hoya carnosa*) and the Hindu rope plant (*Hoya carnosa* var. *compacta*), can tolerate 40–50 per cent, although they'll flourish in higher humidity. Others may require much higher humidity levels, so it's a good idea to check their specific needs when purchasing to ensure that you can provide the right conditions.

Choice species of wax flowers

Porcelain flower
(*Hoya carnosa*)

It's a low-maintenance, fast-growing twiner with succulent, glossy leaves and highly perfumed, pastel pink, star-shaped blooms. *Hoya carnosa* 'Tricolor' has variegated leaves in shades of pink, white and green, while *Hoya carnosa* 'Splash' features deep green leaves with white flecks.

Hindu rope plant
(*Hoya carnosa* var. *compacta*)

I love the twisted foliage on this plant. It's a slow grower, but eventually the vines will spill down the side of the pot and show off their curly locks. It provides an unusual textural contrast to your plant collection.

Sweetheart hoya
(*Hoya kerrii*)

This has adorable, heart-shaped leaves. Often sold as a single leaf in a pot for a fun Valentine's Day gift, it's best to avoid this form if you want a full-sized plant because it will forever remain a leaf. *Hoya kerrii* 'Speckles' offers variegation in shades of cream and green, while *Hoya kerrii* 'Albomarginata' features creamy white edges.

Fishtail hoya
(*Hoya polyneura*)

The common name relates to the shape of the paired leaves, which resembles the tail of a fish. It features light green leaves with prominent dark green veins. The vines cascade beautifully over the edge of the pot, making it a stunning statement piece in a hanging basket.

Common problems of wax flowers

Yellowing leaves, poor growth

Symptom
The leaves are turning yellow, and growth is either stagnant or declining. You may see small foreign bodies on the leaves or stems, accompanied by a sticky residue.

Cause
Sap-sucking pests, or the plant is root-bound.

Solution
Wax flowers are prone to sap-sucking insects, such as aphids, scale and mealybugs. These pests feed on sap, depriving the plant of essential nutrients. Although small, they're visible to the naked eye. They secrete a sticky, sugary substance called honeydew, which attracts ants and encourages the growth of sooty mould, a fungal disease. If the leaves feel sticky, then it's a sign of infestation. To treat these pests, use a horticultural oil or a systemic insecticide.

While wax flowers prefer to remain in the same pot for a few years, over time their roots can occupy most of the available space, reducing air pockets and hindering the efficient uptake of water and nutrients. This can lead to yellowing leaves and stunted growth. Repot the plant into fresh potting mix, but move up only one pot size.

Growing tips

Encourage more flowers
When your wax flower finishes blooming, the individual blossoms will naturally drop. While it might be tempting to tidy up the plant by removing the peduncle (stalk) and spur (knobbly structure on top of the peduncle) where the flowers were attached, resist the urge. Wax flowers rebloom from the same spur year after year. Removing it forces the plant to grow a new one, delaying future flowers. Instead, leave the peduncle and spur intact, and maintain your regular care routine to encourage more flowers next season.

RENAISSANCE DRAWINGS from the UFFIZI
ANSELM KIEFER
PAUL CELAN
CUBIST
PICASSO

Prayer plant

Maranta leuconeura

Care
Low maintenance

Pet friendly
Yes

Light
Bright, indirect light

While many plants in the Marantaceae family are commonly referred to as prayer plants, *Maranta leuconeura* is a standout. Its unique leaf patterns in various colours as well as the way its leaves fold up at night, resembling hands in prayer, make it an iconic representative of the group.

The oval-shaped leaves often feature prominent veins that can be dark green, red or white, creating a striking contrast against the varying shades of green on the surface of the leaves. Some cultivars feature intricate designs that look like fishbones, while others display a marbled or mottled appearance. This incredible range in patterning is perfect for adding texture and depth to your indoor collection.

In its native environment of the tropical rainforests of Central and South America, the prayer plant grows in the understorey, where it thrives in dappled light, warmth and high humidity. It spreads horizontally along the forest floor; when grown as an indoor plant, it will eventually trail lightly over the side of the pot. While this may create a slightly messy appearance, a quick prune can help to maintain its compact shape and bushy habit. Keep the cuttings because they strike easily in water and can be used to propagate new plants or to make your existing plant bushier.

The prayer plant is perfect on a desk, dining table, side table or any surface where you can appreciate the beauty of its leaves - provided you give it the right light, of course!

All the dirt on the prayer plant

Light
The prayer plant grows best in bright, indirect light. It can tolerate lower light conditions, but its leaves will become less vibrant.

Potting mix
Use a moist, well-drained potting mix. I like to combine one part premium potting mix with one part coco peat and one part perlite.

Fertiliser
Liquid feed regularly during the warmer months, or apply a controlled-release fertiliser at the beginning of spring, reapplying as directed.

Water
Water when the top 2.5-5 centimetres (1-2 inches) of potting mix is dry. Ensure that the water runs through the drainage holes at the bottom of the pot.

Humidity
The prayer plant prefers humidity to be around 60-80 per cent, although it will tolerate lower levels of humidity. If the humidity dips too low, then the leaf edges will brown. Keep the plant away from heaters and air conditioners. Group it with other plants to increase humidity, or sit it on a tray filled with pebbles and water. For other ways to boost indoor humidity, see page 26.

Choice cultivars of the prayer plant

***Maranta leuconeura* 'Kerchoveana'**

The pale green leaves have dark black-brown patches along the centre, creating a beautiful contrast. It particularly stands out when paired or grouped with mostly green plants. There's a variegated version, too, featuring bands and specks of creamy white randomly scattered across the leaves.

Maranta leuconeura* var. *erythroneura

This is one gorgeous indoor plant! The velvety leaves feature stunning deep red to pink, herringbone-like veins that contrast beautifully against the dark green surface. It's vibrant and eye-catching, and it will add a striking focal point to your collection.

Growing tips

Trim for tidiness
Over time, the prayer plant will develop a 'skirt' of dead, brown foliage around its base. This is normal, provided that the plant is healthy. However, if you find it unsightly, then you can use a sharp pair of secateurs to trim it off and keep the plant looking tidy.

Common problems of the prayer plant

Browning leaves

Symptom
Browning of the leaf tips.

Cause
This is often a sign of low humidity. It can happen when the plant is exposed to draughts or hot and cool air.

Solution
Position the plant away from open windows and doors, or any other sources of draughts. Additionally, keep it clear of heating or cooling vents. To maintain consistent moisture, consider placing a shallow tray of water near the plant to increase humidity. For other ways to boost indoor humidity, see page 26.

Curling leaves

Symptom
Leaves curled or rolled inwards.

Cause
Insufficient moisture in the potting mix causes the leaves to roll this way to conserve moisture.

Solution
Give the plant a good soak, ensuring that the water runs through the drainage holes at the bottom of the pot. The plant will recover, but be mindful to maintain consistent watering to prevent further stress. Always water when the top 2.5–5 centimetres (1–2 inches) of potting mix is dry.

White fluff and sticky leaves

Symptom
Soft, white tufts resembling cotton are visible in the leaf joints and along the stems, with a sticky residue on the leaves.

Cause
Mealybugs (sap-sucking pests). The sticky residue is honeydew, a by-product of mealybugs.

Solution
Spray affected plant parts with an insecticidal soap. This is a contact insecticide, so ensure that the pests are thoroughly covered for effective control. Repeat sprays may be needed, especially with severe infestations.

Monsteras

Monstera spp.

Care
Low to high maintenance

Pet friendly
No

Light
Bright, indirect light

These will always be some of my favourite plants. The large, lush, heart-shaped, glossy green leaves with slits or holes (fenestrations) are beautiful to observe, and their dramatic and wild stature - once mature - easily livens up any indoor space. The variegated forms are particularly striking and often considered collector's items; thankfully, the eye-watering price of these has significantly reduced over the last few years.

There are several monstera species, ranging from large-leaved forms such as the fruit salad plant (*Monstera deliciosa*) to daintier, trailing types such as the Swiss cheese vine (*Monstera adansonii*).

An interesting trait among many members of the *Monstera* genus is their heteroblastic growth, where juvenile leaves remain relatively small and simple, often without fenestrations, until the plant climbs up a surface. As the leaves mature, they can undergo striking transformations. For example, the fruit salad plant (*Monstera deliciosa*) starts with small, heart-shaped leaves; these eventually develop the iconic split and fenestrated pattern as the plant grows. Similarly, the Swiss cheese vine (*Monstera adansonii*) begins with simple, small leaves; as these mature, they develop into large, perforated foliage. The shingle plant (*Monstera dubia*) begins with intricately patterned, shingling leaves that later transform into larger, solid green leaves with fenestrations, losing their shingling habit as they mature. This change in leaf structure reflects the plant's adaptation to its climbing lifestyle.

Monsteras are native to various tropical regions of Central America, where they thrive in warm, humid conditions and dappled light. They are hemiepiphytic plants, meaning they often start life on the ground before using aerial roots to climb nearby trees. As they grow upward, their lower stems and roots may die back, causing them to lose contact with the soil. At this point, they become epiphytic, using their aerial roots to anchor themselves and absorb nutrients and moisture from the air or tree bark.

All the dirt on monsteras

Light

Monsteras grow best in bright, indirect light. However, I've found that the fruit salad plant (*Monstera deliciosa*) is one of the most adaptable species - it can grow in direct sun outdoors after a period of acclimatisation, but the leaves often burn and become quite tattered on days with extreme heat.

Potting mix

The fruit salad plant (*Monstera deliciosa*) is well suited to a premium potting mix, but most other monsteras prefer a moist, well-drained mix. I like to blend two parts premium potting mix, two parts orchid bark, one part coco chips, one part perlite and one part horticultural charcoal. You can also use a specialty aroid potting mix from your local nursery or garden centre. Alternatively, there are many recipes online, so see what works for you.

Fertiliser

Liquid feed regularly during the warmer months, or apply a controlled-release fertiliser at the beginning of spring, reapplying as directed.

Water

Water when the top 2.5–5 centimetres (1–2 inches) of potting mix is dry. Ensure that the water runs through the drainage holes at the bottom of the pot.

Humidity

The fruit salad plant (*Monstera deliciosa*) and the Swiss cheese vine (*Monstera adansonii*) are happy with the standard level of humidity found in most homes. The variegated forms, such as *Monstera deliciosa* 'Thai Constellation', and other species such as the shingle plant (*Monstera dubia*) prefer higher humidity levels, ideally over 70 per cent, otherwise their leaf edges will start to brown and crisp. For ways to boost indoor humidity, see page 26.

Choice species and cultivars of monsteras

Swiss cheese vine
(*Monstera adansonii*)

The small, heart-shaped leaves with holes are simply adorable! You can let the vine trail gracefully over the side of the pot, or give it a support to climb. With a moss pole and the right growing conditions, the foliage will become larger and more impressive as the plant matures. There are also beautiful variegated forms available in white and mint.

Monstera deliciosa
'Thai Constellation'

This cultivar has splashes or speckles of white that resemble a constellation. It originated from a natural mutation and was selectively cultivated for its unique appearance. Unlike other variegated forms, such as *Monstera deliciosa* var. *albo variegata*, which may revert back to green if the variegation is weak, *Monstera deliciosa* 'Thai Constellation' is known for its stable variegation, ensuring that its leaves consistently display their distinctive pattern.

Shingle plant
(*Monstera dubia*)

Its leaves grow flat along a surface, creating an unusual shingling effect as it climbs. The dark green, highly patterned leaves with silver highlights overlap as they grow. Once mature, the leaves lose their shingling habit and develop fenestrations. The silver markings eventually fade with new leaves.

Common problems of monsteras

Silvery or bronzed foliage

Symptom
Leaves have a silvery or bronzed look, typically on the underside but also on the upper surface. If you look carefully, you can see tiny, yellow, white or black insects crawling on the leaves. Small black droppings are usually scattered over the leaf surfaces.

Cause
Thrips (sap-sucking insects).

Solution
Treat with an insecticidal soap or suitable pesticide. Check the label for instructions, and use only as directed. Repeat treatments may be required. Damage on affected leaves is irreversible, but new growth will be unaffected if successfully treated.

Too many roots

Symptom
Roots randomly appear along the plant.

Cause
Aerial roots are natural growths along the plant's stem that search for a surface or support to cling to and climb.

Solution
You don't need to take any action with these growths. However, if you find them unsightly, then you can tuck the ends of the roots into the potting mix to encourage them to grow downwards. This can help to stabilise the plant, especially if it's top heavy. Alternatively, trim the excess roots from the stem using a clean, sharp pair of secateurs or a blade.

Growing tips

Tame a wild plant
A monstera naturally wants to climb, but if it doesn't have a support, then it will trail over the pot. This can look messy, especially for larger species. To encourage it to stay upright, you can simply tie stems to stakes or use a tomato grow cage.

Alternatively, provide the plant with a moss pole or support system for the aerial roots to cling to; this will encourage it to grow upwards and develop larger leaves. To make your own moss pole, grab a growing medium (such as sphagnum moss, orchid bark or tree fern fibre) plus wire cutters, wire mesh and cable ties, then follow these step-by-step instructions:

1. Use wire cutters to cut a piece of wire mesh so it's wide enough to form a cylinder approximately 6 centimetres (2 ⅓ inches) in diameter and your desired length – typically 30 centimetres (12 inches), 60 centimetres (24 inches) or 90 centimetres (36 inches).
2. If you're using sphagnum moss, then soak it in water and squeeze out the excess.
3. Lay the mesh flat. Spread the sphagnum moss evenly along one end of the mesh, leaving approximately 10 centimetres (4 inches) of the bottom end of the mesh free from moss.
4. Roll the mesh around the sphagnum moss, ensuring that the moss is evenly distributed and not too tightly packed. Make sure that the mesh cylinder maintains a consistent diameter along the length.
5. Secure the mesh with cable ties, spacing them evenly along the cylinder to hold the sphagnum moss in place.
6. Place the mesh cylinder into an empty pot, and fill the bottom of the cylinder with potting mix for stability. Position the plant, then backfill the pot with potting mix.
7. Use garden ties to loosely secure the plant to the mesh cylinder, making sure that nodes or aerial roots make contact with the sphagnum moss. Press down on the top of the potting mix to stabilise the plant.

If you're using orchid bark or tree fern fibre, then roll the mesh to form a cylinder, secure the ends with cable ties, and place the cylinder into the pot before filling it with your desired growing medium. Pot up the plant, and use garden ties to loosely secure the plant to the mesh cylinder.

You can also buy premade poles or other support systems that simply need filling with the growing medium of your choice. All of them work well; it will come down to cost and personal preference.

Boston fern

Nephrolepis exaltata

Care
Low maintenance

Pet friendly
Yes

Light
Bright, indirect light

The Boston fern is the go-to species for those who have struggled to grow maidenhair ferns or other finicky varieties. The voluminous, feathery fronds and lush green foliage also draw many people to this plant. With its resilience and relatively easy-care nature, it's a popular and forgiving choice for both novice and experienced plant enthusiasts alike.

I can definitely attest to its forgiving nature. I once brought mine outside – although I can't remember why – and left it hanging in a sheltered corner. It only got the odd bit of rain or hose water, and over time it slowly dropped its leaflets. Yet it still hung in there, sprouting new fronds while others died back. It didn't look its best, but it wasn't dead! Eventually, I cut back the straggly fronds, moved it to a better spot inside, and it bounced back to its former voluptuous self.

It's sometimes seen as an 'old-fashioned' plant, as it enjoyed great popularity in the nineteenth century, particularly during the Victorian era, when it was often displayed on a decorative plant stand or in a hanging basket. During this time, ferneries – specialised spaces or greenhouses dedicated to the cultivation of ferns – were all the rage, with the Boston fern being a central feature. However, as the saying goes, what's old is new again, and this fern is making a comeback, bringing its lush locks and timeless charm into our modern homes.

The Boston fern is native to tropical and subtropical regions, thriving in humid forests, near swamps and along riverbeds. While it's adaptable to most indoor environments, it can also flourish in the right spot on a patio. With the proper balance of light and moisture, your fern will be happy and healthy.

All the dirt on the Boston fern

Light
The Boston fern grows best in bright, indirect light. While it can tolerate medium light, this will result in sparse fronds and often leaf drop.

Potting mix
Use a specialty fern blend, or mix your own by combining equal parts premium potting mix, perlite or coarse sand, and coco peat.

Fertiliser
Feed regularly with an indoor plant fertiliser when the fern is actively growing, typically during spring and summer.

Water
Water regularly to keep the potting mix moist but not wet. Insert your finger 2.5–5 centimetres (1–2 inches) into the potting mix. If the mix is moist, then leave watering for a few days; if it's dry, then give the plant a good drink. Reduce watering frequency in winter when the Boston fern's growth slows.

Humidity
The Boston fern loves humidity and thrives when it's 50–80 per cent. If the air is too dry, then their fronds may begin to brown and shed. For ways to boost indoor humidity, see page 26.

Choice cultivars of the Boston fern

Nephrolepis exaltata
'Fluffy Ruffles'

As the name suggests, this fern has adorable fronds that are both fluffy and ruffly. With its compact size, reaching only about 30 centimetres (12 inches) tall and 60 centimetres (24 inches) wide, it's a handy smaller alternative to the traditional Boston fern.

Nephrolepis exaltata
'Variegata'

I love the variegation on this cultivar - the individual leaflets feature random yellow stripes, with some entirely yellow and others completely green. This mix creates a unique and delightful appearance, making the fern a real standout in any collection.

Common problems of the Boston fern

Leaf shed

Symptom
Leaves dry out and turn brown, followed by shedding.

Cause
If the humidity is too low, the potting mix becomes too dry, or the fern is exposed to cold conditions, then the fern may react by dropping leaves as a stress response.

Solution
To keep your Boston fern healthy and fully foliaged, ensure that both the humidity and the potting mix moisture are well maintained. Avoid exposing the fern to draughts or sudden drops in temperature. To tidy up the fern, remove spent fronds by cutting them back to ground level, and give it a gentle shake to dislodge any loose leaflets. With the right care, new fronds will grow.

Growing tips

Save your fading Boston fern
Even if your Boston fern has suffered from neglect, pests or diseases, you may be able to salvage it. Begin by removing the plant from its pot and checking the roots. Healthy roots should be firm and neither completely dried out nor rotten. If the roots are in good condition and there are signs of life (such as some leaflets that refuse to die), then the plant is likely to recover.

Trim back all of the fronds to near ground level using a sharp pair of secateurs. If the existing potting mix is old and compacted, then repot into fresh mix. However, if the potting mix looks fine, then skip repotting. Reposition the pruned plant in a spot with bright, indirect light, and water regularly to keep the potting mix consistently moist.

Purple shamrock

Oxalis triangularis

Care
Low maintenance

Pet friendly
No

Light
Bright, indirect light

I remember the first time I saw the purple shamrock. It was at the Collectors' Plant Fair in Clarendon, Sydney, and I was immediately captivated by its delicate, two-toned-purple leaves on slender, wispy stems that resembled floating butterflies. Unfortunately, they had sold out by the time I decided to buy one. Note to self: always purchase stunning plants at first sight! Luckily, I was able to track one down after the fair. Back then, they weren't readily available, but now they're easier to find.

The vibrant purple leaves provide a striking colour contrast to the various shades of green found in an indoor plant collection. An interesting feature of this plant is its daily rhythm: the leaves fold up at night and then unfold gracefully in the morning as they soak up the light. It has sweet, lilac-coloured flowers during the warmer months, but they also appear at other times of the year, depending on the growing conditions.

Oxalis species grow from corms (underground bulb-like structures) that multiply over the years, resulting in a bushy specimen. These corms can be lifted and divided to make new plants for you or for sharing with friends, or they can be simply left in the pot. After a few years, you may want to lift and repot the corms to give them more room to grow.

In cooler climates, the leaves and stems typically die back as the plant enters dormancy, but the corms will reshoot once the weather warms in spring. If your indoor environment remains above 18 degrees Celsius (64 degrees Fahrenheit) during winter, then the plant may not become dormant, allowing you to enjoy its lush foliage all year round.

All the dirt on the purple shamrock

Light
The purple shamrock grows best in bright, indirect light. A few hours of direct sun in the morning is ideal if you can manage it. If the light is uneven, then you'll notice the stems leaning towards the source. To maintain even growth, rotate the plant every few weeks.

Potting mix
Combine two parts premium potting mix and one part perlite.

Fertiliser
Liquid feed regularly during the warmer months, or apply a controlled-release fertiliser at the beginning of spring, reapplying as directed.

Water
Water when the top 2.5-5 centimetres (1-2 inches) of potting mix is dry.

Humidity
The purple shamrock is not particularly fussy about humidity and will adapt to the standard level of humidity found in most homes.

Common problems of the purple shamrock

Yellow-orange, powdery spots on leaves

Symptom
Small, yellow-orange, powdery spots are seen on the underside of leaves, which may fall. The plant looks unhealthy.

Cause
Rust (fungal infection).

Solution
Remove the worst-affected leaves, and spray the remainder of the plant with a fungicide containing myclobutanil (systemic) or lime sulphur (contact). If you prefer not to use chemicals, then cut back the plant to ground level; with regular watering and access to bright, indirect light, it will eventually reshoot.

Dying back

Symptom
Leaves and stems are wilting and dying back, typically during winter.

Cause
Oxalis species naturally become dormant in winter as temperatures drop and daylight hours reduce. During this time, the plant will die back to its corms, storing energy for regrowth in the warmer months. (Note that if indoor temperatures remain above 18 degrees Celsius [64 degrees Fahrenheit] and the plant is positioned in a warm, brightly lit spot, then it may not enter dormancy at all.)

Solution
While the plant is dormant, reduce watering significantly; allow the potting mix to dry out between waterings to avoid root rot. Once new growth appears, you can gradually resume regular watering.

Growing tips

Propagate your purple shamrock
If you'd like to create new plants for your indoor garden or share your purple shamrock with friends, then the process is super simple. When the plant loses its leaves and enters dormancy in late winter, tip the potting mix out of the pot and search for the corms (pale salmon-coloured, scaly, bulb-like structures). Gently separate them and dust off any remaining potting mix. Fill smaller pots with potting mix, and plant the corms 2.5–5 centimetres (1–2 inches) deep, with the narrower end pointing up. Water in lightly, then water sparingly to prevent the corms from drying out.

If your plant doesn't enter dormancy, then it's best to divide the plant when it's actively growing during spring and summer. Gently remove the plant from its pot, use your hands to divide it into equal sections (ensuring that each section has healthy roots and stems), and plant the sections into new pots with fresh potting mix. Water in well.

Peperomias

Peperomia spp.

Care
Low to high maintenance

Pet friendly
Yes

Light
Bright, indirect light

There is immense diversity in this genus of over 1000 species, many of which are popular houseplants. The variety includes a range of interesting foliage forms and textures, from thick, rubbery leaves to delicate foliage with intricate patterns. The good news is that many of these plants are compact, so they don't take up much room – meaning you can enjoy more plants in your space!

Peperomias are native to warm, humid environments in tropical and subtropical regions of Central and South America. They'll thrive indoors if the conditions are similar to those in their native habitats. While many peperomias are relatively low maintenance, some species require more care. If you're aiming for a low-maintenance experience, then it's wise to choose your species carefully.

Group a few of them together for an eye-catching display, particularly a mix of emerald ripple peperomia (*Peperomia caperata*) cultivars. Alternatively, the diverse array of colours and patterns found in peperomias can easily be combined with other greenery, creating arrangements that offer both complementary and contrasting elements. Within the genus, you'll also find compact, bushy plants and trailing varieties, allowing you to play with height and texture in your plant arrangements.

All the dirt on peperomias

Light
Peperomias prefer bright, indirect light but can tolerate lower light conditions. However, prolonged periods of low light may cause leaf shedding and a loss of variegation.

Potting mix
Use a moist, well-drained potting mix, such as two parts premium potting mix blended with one part perlite to assist with drainage.

Fertiliser
Every month from spring to summer, you can apply a liquid fertiliser that has been diluted to half strength. Alternatively, apply a controlled-release fertiliser at the beginning of spring.

Water
Water when the top 2.5–5 centimetres (1–2 inches) of potting mix is dry. Ensure that the water runs through the drainage holes at the bottom of the pot.

Humidity
Peperomias have varying humidity preferences. Most are adaptable to the standard level of humidity found in most homes, while some prefer it to be slightly higher. Regardless of their specific needs, it's best to keep peperomias away from draughts to maintain a stable environment.

Choice species and cultivars of peperomias

Watermelon peperomia (*Peperomia argyreia*)

Its rounded, teardrop-shaped leaves adorned with striking blue-green and silvery markings resemble little watermelons, and the deep red stems complete the look. The combination of these features makes it irresistibly cute! Take care not to overwater, and keep it in a warm spot - it detests cold draughts! *Peperomia argyreia* 'Silver' boasts more pronounced silver and narrower green markings. *Peperomia argyreia* 'Variegata' has creamy white and green patterns.

Emerald ripple peperomia (*Peperomia caperata*)

There are several cultivars of this species, each as mesmerising as the next. All feature deeply ridged leaves with a wavy texture, but the foliage comes in a variety of colours: dark green, silver-green, mottled cream and silver-grey, pink, deep burgundy, and so on.

Baby rubber plant (*Peperomia obtusifolia*)

A hardy, low-maintenance peperomia, it has fleshy stems and leathery, glossy green leaves. Its bushy, upright, compact habit makes it an excellent choice for a shallow pot; place a few together for an eye-catching display. You can also find attractive variegated forms, including *Peperomia obtusifolia* 'Golden Gate', *Peperomia obtusifolia* 'Albo-marginata' and *Peperomia obtusifolia* 'Lemon Lime'.

String of turtles (*Peperomia prostrata*)

This sweet peperomia has tiny, disc-like leaves marked with intricate, red-brown patterns resembling a turtle's shell. As the leaves mature, the venation transitions to silvery white. Avoid overwatering, as the thin stems rot easily if they're kept too moist.

***Peperomia scandens* 'Variegata'**

A trailing peperomia, it has variegated green and creamy white, heart-shaped foliage. It's a low-maintenance plant that thrives with minimal care, and it makes a wonderful specimen in a hanging basket or elevated on a plant stand where its dangling vines can be showcased.

Common problems of peperomias

Wilted and shedding stems

Symptom
Stems are rotting at the base, which causes them to collapse and fall off.

Cause
Overwatering.

Solution
Remove the affected stems to prevent the spread of rot. Change your routine so you only water when the top 2.5-5 centimetres (1-2 inches) of potting mix is dry. Ensure that the potting mix drains well and the pot has holes in the bottom.

Growing tips

Propagate your peperomias
Peperomias are some of the easiest plants to propagate - you can use a leaf or stem cutting.

For leaf cuttings, select a healthy leaf and cut it off at the base of the stem, snipping the stem close to the leaf. Slice horizontally across the leaf, close to the stem end, and place the cut side down into a propagating mix (a blend of one part general potting mix and one part perlite or washed river sand) or moistened sphagnum moss. Position the cutting in a warm, bright spot out of direct sun. Roots will develop over time, then baby plants will begin to grow from the base of the leaf.

For stem cuttings, snip off a healthy stem and leaf, and place the cut end in water. Keep it in a warm spot with bright, indirect light, and change the water every few days, ensuring that the base of the stem is submerged. Roots will develop over time, then baby plants will begin to grow from the base of the stem.

Moth orchids

Phalaenopsis spp.

Care
Medium maintenance

Pet friendly
Yes

Light
Bright, indirect light

There are thousands of moth orchid hybrid cultivars, and the extensive breeding within this genus has led to a vast array of different flower colours, patterns and sizes. They're readily available at nurseries, garden centres, supermarkets and florists, and their flowers look fabulous. So, they make excellent gifts for friends, family members and acquaintances. Plus, the flowers last for a while - often months - providing beauty and interest for an extended period of time.

Unfortunately, once the flowers fade, many moth orchids are discarded or neglected. Unbeknown to their owners, these orchids can produce - with the right care - stunning blooms again, and they'll continue to do so for many years to come.

The common name comes from the appearance of the flowers, which are said to resemble moths in flight. Despite being easily startled by flying insects, I'm certainly happy to be surrounded by these 'moths'!

Moth orchid species are native to several regions in Asia and Australia, where they grow in warm, humid and tropical environments, often as epiphytes on trees or as lithophytes on rocks. They use their roots to anchor themselves and also to absorb moisture and nutrients from the air, rain or surrounding surfaces. Thankfully, they've adapted to most home environments, without the need to be mounted onto a tree or rock.

All the dirt on moth orchids

Light
Moth orchids need a brightly lit position to thrive, especially if you want to encourage flowering. Don't place them in direct sun, otherwise the foliage will burn, and avoid low-light rooms.

Potting mix
Use sphagnum moss or orchid bark. Sphagnum moss can hold a significant amount of water, ensuring that there is consistent moisture for the roots, but its loose structure also allows for good air circulation around the roots.

Fertiliser
Feed regularly with an orchid-specific fertiliser when the leaves and flowers are actively growing.

Water
Insert your finger 2.5-5 centimetres (1-2 inches) into the growing medium, and feel if it's moist or dry before watering. Moth orchids can be watered with tap water, rainwater or distilled water. If your orchid is sitting in a decorative outer pot, it's best to remove it from the pot before watering. Take it over to the sink, run water over the growing medium, and allow it to drain freely. Sit it in the sink for a few minutes to allow any excess water to drain before returning the plant to its outer pot. Reduce watering frequency in winter.

Humidity
Moth orchids thrive with 60-80 per cent humidity. Many people place their orchids in the bathroom, thinking it's a high-humidity environment, but the humidity only increases during and a short time after a shower. Dry leaf tips, wrinkled foliage or dropping buds are all signs that the humidity may be too low. For ways to boost indoor humidity, see page 26.

Common problems of moth orchids

Yellowing, soft leaves

Symptom
Yellowing leaves, mushy brown roots, and leaf or flower loss.

Cause
Overwatering or poor drainage.

Solution
Remove the affected plant parts, and take the plant out of the pot. Inspect the roots – healthy roots are firm and green, while rotten roots are brown and mushy, and emit a foul odour. If most of the roots are rotten, then it's best to discard the plant. However, if the majority of the roots are healthy, then trim the affected roots, sterilising the secateurs after each cut to avoid spreading pathogens. Repot the plant into a fresh growing medium, water well, and position in a spot with bright, indirect light.

If you notice that a moth orchid's leaves are yellowing, but there are no other symptoms and the plant appears otherwise healthy, then it's likely just the natural ageing process at work. Orchids can shed older leaves as they grow. However, if quite a few leaves are turning yellow at the same time, then you may need to investigate further.

Soft, wrinkled leaves

Symptom
Limp, wrinkled leaves.

Cause
Insufficient water.

Solution
Water the plant, and see how it responds. It should typically bounce back within the week. If it doesn't, then there may be an issue with the roots. In such cases, remove the plant from its pot, trim away any dead or damaged roots, and repot into a fresh growing medium.

Choice species of moth orchids

Moon orchid
(*Phalaenopsis amabilis*)

This species has beautiful, pure white blooms with yellow and red patterning on the flower throat. It's often used in hybridisation for the elegance of its white flowers.

Black/brown spots on leaves

Symptom
Small, black/brown, water-soaked lesions on leaves, which may be surrounded by a green-yellow halo. Infected areas enlarge and spread, and they may ooze a foul, bacteria-laden liquid.

Cause
Bacterial brown spot (*Acidovorax* spp.) or bacterial brown rot (*Erwinia* spp.). Pathogens enter via wounds and easily spread via water splash.

Solution
Remove affected leaves, sterilising the secateurs after each cut, and promptly bin the foliage. A liquid copper solution, such as copper oxychloride, may also help with control.

White, cotton-like fluff or dust

Symptom
Cottony fluff around the base of the plant, on the underside of leaves or on flowers, often accompanied by a sticky residue. Affected leaves turn yellow and become floppy. In severe cases, the plant may show stunted growth or overall poor health.

Cause
Mealybugs (sap-sucking insects).

Solution
Spray affected parts thoroughly with an insecticidal soap. A horticultural oil can also be effective, but moth orchids may be sensitive to oils, so test on a small, inconspicuous spot first. Observe over a few days to see if there are any adverse reactions, such as browning or dieback. If there are no reactions, then you can proceed with a more widespread spray.

Growing tips

Encourage repeat flowering
Once the first flowers for the season have faded and dropped off, use a sharp pair of secateurs to cut the stem back to above the first node. Continue to care for the plant as usual, and this should encourage another flower stem to form. If the stem becomes straw-coloured or dries out, then cut it off at the base. Hopefully, this will encourage a healthy new flower stem to form.

Philodendrons

Philodendron spp.

Care
Low to high maintenance

Pet friendly
No

Light
Bright, indirect light

Philodendrons will always have a place in my home. Many years ago, I was gifted a *Philodendron* 'Rojo Congo' by my partner, who was misled into believing it was a rare plant and consequently paid way more than you ever would for this cultivar. He doesn't know anything about plants, so he relied on the word of the seller. I'll always treasure it, but it still makes me annoyed sometimes when I think about how he was conned!

Anyway, there is so much variety when it comes to philodendrons. From larger-than-life specimens to more compact, smaller-leaved forms, there is a diverse range of options to suit your home. Easy-care plants include *Philodendron* 'Rojo Congo' and the heart-leaf philodendron (*Philodendron hederaceum*), while others - such as *Philodendron ilsemanii* and *Philodendron* 'Whipple Way' - require more attention, thriving in warmer conditions and higher humidity. I daresay there's a philodendron to suit every display need, whether it's in a hanging basket, on a shelf or positioned as a stately floor plant.

One fascinating botanical trait exhibited by many philodendrons is heteroblasty. This means that they can produce leaves of different shapes or sizes at various stages of growth. A striking example is the red bristle philodendron (*Philodendron squamiferum*). Its juvenile leaves are smooth and undivided, while the mature leaves develop deep lobes - it's a dramatic transformation.

All the dirt on philodendrons

Light
Philodendrons grow best in bright, indirect light. While some can cope with lower light conditions, their growth will slow; variegated varieties might lose their distinctive patterns.

Potting mix
Use an aroid potting mix, which you might find as a bagged product at your local nursery or garden centre. Alternatively, create your own aroid potting mix by blending two parts premium potting mix, two parts orchid bark, one part coco chips, one part perlite and one part horticultural charcoal.

Fertiliser
Liquid feed regularly during the warmer months, or apply a controlled-release fertiliser at the beginning of spring, reapplying as directed.

Water
Water when the top 2.5–5 centimetres (1–2 inches) of potting mix is dry. Ensure that the water runs through the drainage holes at the bottom of the pot.

Humidity
Philodendrons have varying humidity preferences. While most thrive in the standard level of humidity found in most homes, some species require higher humidity, often around 60 per cent or more, otherwise their leaves will start to brown and crisp. For ways to boost indoor humidity, see page 26.

Choice species and cultivars of philodendrons

***Philodendron erubescens* 'Pink Princess'**

I think most of the world has fallen in love with this cultivar, especially plant enthusiasts who adore the colour pink. Leaves emerge pink before gradually maturing to a deep green with prominent pink variegation. It prefers to climb but can also trail.

Creeping velvet philodendron (*Philodendron gloriosum*)

You'll be captivated, just as I was, by the lush, velvety leaves and striking white veins on this philodendron. It has a crawling habit, so tends to grow along the ground rather than climb. Place it in a small trough, and you'll see it spread horizontally; in a regular pot it will simply trail over the side.

Silver sword philodendron (*Philodendron hastatum*)

A stunning plant, it has silvery blue-green foliage. The juvenile leaves are spear-shaped, and they eventually mature to lobed, sword-like shapes. Train it to climb up a moss pole, or allow it to trail wildly over the edge of a pot.

Heart-leaf philodendron (*Philodendron hederaceum*)

A classic philodendron, it has heart-shaped leaves growing on vines. Give it a support such as a moss pole, and it will climb; otherwise, the vines will gently hang over the side of the pot. You can find variegated forms, such as *Philodendron hederaceum* 'Brasil' and *Philodendron hederaceum* 'Cream Splash'. There's also a velvet-textured form, *Philodendron hederaceum* var. *hederaceum* 'Micans'.

***Philodendron* 'Rojo Congo'**

It has a compact, bushy habit, often referred to as self-heading. The leaves emerge with a captivating coppery red hue, gradually maturing to a deep burgundy, before eventually settling into a rich dark green. The plant's stems are also vibrant red, adding to its overall visual appeal. This low-maintenance plant is suitable for beginners.

Red bristle philodendron (*Philodendron squamiferum*)

While every philodendron is unique, this one stands out for its unusual features. I adore its fuzzy red stems, which create a striking contrast against its deeply lobed, dark green leaves. As the plant matures, the leaf lobes become even more pronounced. Being a climber, it benefits from a support but can also gracefully trail over the edge of a pot.

Common problems of philodendrons

Silvery, mottled leaves

Symptom
Leaves have a silvery, mottled appearance. Leaf edges may yellow, and fine webbing may be observed between the leaves and stems.

Cause
Spider mites (sap-sucking arachnids).

Solution
Remove the worst-affected leaves, and treat the plant with an insecticidal soap, horticultural oil (such as neem oil or white oil) or suitable miticide (such as products containing abamectin). Always follow the label instructions carefully.

Small brown or white bumps on leaves

Symptom
Brown, white, black or coloured bumps on leaves and stems. They can be easily scratched off with your fingernail. The affected plant parts may also be covered in a sticky residue.

Cause
Scale (sap-sucking insects).

Solution
Treat with a horticultural oil because it coats their waxy shells and suffocates them. Alternatively, look for a systemic insecticide that targets sap-sucking insects, or carefully dab a cotton bud soaked in rubbing alcohol directly onto the pests.

Growing tips

Encourage upward growth
Most philodendrons have a climbing habit. You can encourage this behaviour indoors by providing your plant with a support (such as a moss or coir pole or tree-fern stake). You can purchase this support or make your own (see page 193).

Insert the support into the back of the pot. If there isn't enough room, then you'll need to repot the plant into a larger container to accommodate the support. Position the stem against the support, ensuring that the nodes are in contact with the support. Use soft garden ties to secure the stem in place. Aerial roots will eventually form at these nodes, helping the plant to stay upright and climb. Regularly moisten the support to encourage aerial roots to attach.

Once the plant outgrows its support, you can either extend the support or 'chop and prop', which involves cutting back the plant to a desired height and repotting the cutting into fresh aroid mix with a new support.

A/B

Chinese money plant

Pilea peperomioides

Care
Low maintenance

Pet friendly
Yes

Light
Bright, indirect light

I remember the *obsession* with this plant. It was all over social media, and people were paying exorbitant prices for even the smallest specimens (myself included!). At the time, it was unlike anything we'd seen before in the plant world. Small to medium-sized, round, dark green, disc-like leaves perch on the ends of slender stems, which delicately emerge from a thin, corky trunk – like something out of a whimsical storybook!

These days, you can find the Chinese money plant in most nurseries and garden centres at a reasonable price. It can grow quite tall, reaching 50–60 centimetres (20–24 inches), and often develops a bare stem with a lush crown of foliage, giving it a tree-like quality. However, it may not stay bare for long – the plant naturally produces little pups around its base. These pups can be either left to fill out the bottom of the mother plant or separated and replanted to create new plants. For this reason, it's also known as the friendship plant or pass-it-on plant, as it's easy to propagate and share with friends.

Initially, the Chinese money plant makes an excellent desk specimen. As it grows taller, however, it may be better on a plant stand or shelf where it won't overwhelm the space. You may need to use a stake to keep it upright as it grows. Attach the plant loosely with a garden tie or piece of jute to avoid strangling it.

All the dirt on the Chinese money plant

Light
The Chinese money plant thrives in bright, indirect light or filtered light. Avoid placing it in direct sun because this can scorch the leaves. It won't tolerate low light, which can result in poor growth, yellowing foliage and leaf drop.

Potting mix
Blend two parts premium potting mix with one part perlite to assist with drainage.

Fertiliser
Liquid feed regularly during the warmer months, or apply a controlled-release fertiliser at the beginning of spring, reapplying as directed.

Water
Water when the top 2.5–5 centimetres (1–2 inches) of potting mix is dry.

Humidity
Any humidity level will do, but if you ensure that it's above 50 per cent, then the Chinese money plant will appreciate it. Keep it away from draughts, and group it with other plants to increase humidity. For other ways to boost indoor humidity, see page 26.

Common problems of the Chinese money plant

Falling leaves

Symptom
Dropping of the lower leaves.

Cause
Insufficient light and/or overwatering.

Solution
The Chinese money plant thrives in bright, indirect light. If it's positioned in low light, then move it to a spot where it can receive more light – but avoid anywhere that receives direct sun, which can scorch the leaves.

Excessive watering can cause the roots to become waterlogged, leading to leaf drop. Ensure that the potting mix drains well, and allow the top 2.5–5 centimetres (1–2 inches) of potting mix to dry out before watering the plant again.

Excessive leaning

Symptom
The plant is tilting to one side.

Cause
The Chinese money plant tends to grow towards the light, especially when the light is unevenly distributed.

Solution
Rotate the plant every couple of weeks to ensure even, upright growth.

Growing tips

Separate and divide pups
Over time, the Chinese money plant may produce pups around its base. Once these reach around 10 centimetres (4 inches) in height, you can carefully separate them from the mother plant. Remove the mother plant from its pot, and gently tease the pups away. If necessary, use a sharp pair of snips or secateurs to cut the roots. Pot the pups into small containers filled with a premium potting mix, and water them in well. Repot the mother plant back into its original pot with fresh potting mix.

Mini monstera

Rhaphidophora tetrasperma

Care
Low maintenance

Pet friendly
No

Light
Bright, indirect light

The mini monstera is not part of the *Monstera* genus, but it is related. It belongs to the Araceae family, which is also home to *Monstera* species. While the mini monstera shares some similarities with its relative, such as attractive foliage, it's distinct in its own right.

The leaves of the mini monstera are bright green and deeply lobed. In ideal conditions, the plant can produce large leaves, but not as huge as those of *Monstera* species. In its native rainforests of Malaysia and southern Thailand, it uses aerial roots to climb up trees. So, in your home, give it a moss pole, stake or trellis for support, otherwise it may grow into a wild mess!

A young plant is perfectly suited to life as a decorative feature on a desk or side table. However, as the plant grows, it will be best displayed on a larger table or on the floor to ensure that it doesn't overwhelm the space.

Like other members of the Araceae family, the mini monstera exhibits heteroblasty: it can have both juvenile and mature leaves on the same plant. The juvenile leaves are smooth and whole, while the mature leaves develop deep lobes. This contrast adds to its visual interest.

All the dirt on the mini monstera

Light
The mini monstera thrives in bright, indirect light. In low-light conditions, growth will slow; the leaves will be smaller and may eventually drop.

Potting mix
Use an aroid potting mix. This typically consists of premium potting mix, perlite, orchid bark, coco peat, coco chips and horticultural charcoal. I often create my own blend of two parts premium potting mix, two parts orchid bark, one part coco chips, one part perlite and one part horticultural charcoal. If you search online, then you'll find countless recipes for creating your own aroid mix. Alternatively, you might find bagged aroid mix at your local nursery or garden centre.

Fertiliser
Liquid feed regularly during the warmer months, or apply a controlled-release fertiliser at the beginning of spring, reapplying as directed.

Water
Water when the top 2.5-5 centimetres (1-2 inches) of potting mix is dry.

Humidity
The mini monstera is happy with the standard level of humidity found in most homes. However, it will appreciate a little more humidity if you can manage it. For ways to boost indoor humidity, see page 26.

Choice cultivar of the mini monstera

Rhaphidophora tetrasperma **'Variegata'**

The bright green leaves feature creamy white blotches or marbling; the variegation extends to the stem, adding to the plant's overall beauty. However, it's a rare find and likely to be quite expensive if you come across one.

Common problems of the mini monstera

Silvery or bronzed foliage

Symptom
Leaves have a silvery or bronzed appearance, typically on the upper surface but can also be on the underside. Fine webbing may be observed between the leaves and stems.

Cause
Spider mites (sap-sucking arachnids).

Solution
Remove the worst-affected leaves, and treat the plant with an insecticidal soap, horticultural oil (such as neem oil or white oil) or suitable miticide (such as products containing abamectin). Always follow the label instructions carefully.

Growing tips

Make your mini monstera climb
Providing your mini monstera with a support will help to keep it tidy and also allow you to appreciate its beautiful leaves. You can use a moss or coir pole - or even small hooks fixed to the wall - to guide the plant up and around the room.

Place the moss or coir pole at the back of the pot, pressing it down into the potting mix to stabilise it. Position the stem against the support, and secure it with garden ties spaced evenly along the stem. Ensure that the nodes make good contact, but don't make the ties too tight because this can damage the stem.

Regularly moisten the surface of the moss or coir to encourage roots to latch on to the support. In most cases, the ties can eventually be removed, but they may be needed to continue to train the stem up the pole.

Lady palm

Rhapis excelsa

Care
Low maintenance

Pet friendly
Yes

Light
Bright, indirect light

The elegant lady palm features handsome, dark green, fan-shaped leaves that emerge from multiple canes, creating a lush, voluminous appearance. The canes are wrapped in coarse, dark brown fibre, which – combined with the deeply creased, textured foliage and blunt leaf tips – gives the plant real character. With its strong presence, this plant works beautifully as a stand-alone feature by the front door or in a cosy corner of the study or living room.

It can eventually reach up to 4 metres (13 feet) tall, but its slow growth means that it will remain compact for quite some time, saving you the hassle of frequent repotting. It prefers to be slightly root-bound.

Interestingly, the lady palm is one of the oldest cultivated palms. It has been prized as an ornamental in Asia since the seventeenth century. The Japanese elite, particularly the shogunate, admired the lady palm as a symbol of status and elegance. Its aesthetic appeal eventually caught the attention of the West, where it became popular for its ease of care, durability and long lifespan.

Available in both green and variegated forms, the lady palm remains a beloved choice for homes. It's tolerant of low light and not particularly fussy about humidity, making it perfect for a wide range of indoor environments.

All the dirt on the lady palm

Light
The lady palm prefers a spot with bright, indirect light. It tolerates medium and low light levels, but this will slow down growth. Avoid direct sun because this can burn the leaves.

Potting mix
Use a moist, well-drained potting mix that's rich in organic matter, such as a blend of three parts premium potting mix, one part perlite and one part compost.

Fertiliser
The lady palm isn't a hungry plant, so there's no need to feed it often. You can apply a controlled-release or slow-release organic fertiliser in spring. Alternatively, dilute a liquid fertiliser to half strength, and apply it once a month during spring and summer.

Water
Water when the top 2.5–5 centimetres (1–2 inches) of potting mix is dry. Ensure that the water runs through the drainage holes at the bottom of the pot.

Humidity
The lady palm is adaptable to the standard level of humidity found in most homes. While it thrives in medium humidity, it can tolerate lower levels without significant stress.

Common problems of the lady palm

Bumps on leaves or stems

Symptom
Small brown, white or coloured bumps on leaves or stems. They can be easily scratched off with your fingernail.

Cause
Scale (sap-sucking insects).

Solution
As scale insects can hide in the fibrous bases of the leaves, it's best to use a systemic insecticide to control these pests. A product containing an active ingredient such as imidacloprid or acetamiprid is absorbed by the plant, making it toxic to pests when they feed on the sap. In contrast, horticultural oil requires direct contact to be effective and can sometimes burn the leaves of sensitive palms, so it isn't the best option for control.

White, dust-like fluff on leaves or stems

Symptom
Cottony fluff scattered on leaves or stems. Affected plant parts may be covered in a sticky residue.

Cause
Mealybugs (sap-sucking insects). The sticky residue is honeydew, a by-product of mealybugs.

Solution
Spray leaves and affected plant parts with an insecticidal soap or systemic pesticide. You can wipe off the sticky residue with a damp microfibre cloth.

Silvery, mottled foliage

Symptom
Silvering of leaf surfaces; webbing may be present.

Cause
Spider mites (sap-sucking arachnids).

Solution
Spray fronds with insecticidal soap or a suitable miticide. Horticultural oil is also effective, but palms are often sensitive to oils – so, proceed with caution.

Brown leaf tips

Symptom
Leaves are turning brown at the tips or edges.

Cause
This is common with *Rhapis* palms and can be caused by underwatering or allowing the plant to dry out too long between waterings.

Solution
Only water the lady palm when the top 2.5–5 centimetres (1–2 inches) of potting mix is dry, ensuring that you provide a thorough soaking. The brown tips won't recover, but you can trim the ends with serrated scissors (or pinking shears) to mimic the plant's natural leaf tip.

Growing tips

Prune to tidy
Over time, the older leaves of the lady palm may naturally discolour and die. You can prune these leaves at the base of the stem to restore the plant's neat and tidy appearance.

Mistletoe cacti

Rhipsalis spp.

Care
Low maintenance

Pet friendly
Yes

Light
Bright, indirect light

The best displays of mistletoe cacti I've ever seen were outdoors, tucked in protected spots under the shade of a tree and on a patio. Both set-ups had the cacti hanging at different heights, creating a layered effect that gave the eyes something to admire at every level. The long, trailing stems of the cacti - each with a unique shape, texture and shade of green - were on full show. With access to bright, indirect light and regular watering, the plants thrived and created a jungle-like feel. Fortunately, mistletoe cacti also make ideal houseplants.

Native to the tropical and subtropical regions of Central and South America, mistletoe cacti grow at altitude as epiphytes, thriving in warm, humid environments nestled in the crooks of trees. In their natural habitat, they endure periods of drought followed by heavy downpours, but indoors, it's best to water them regularly, especially during the warmer months.

For a dynamic display that creates vertical interest, try hanging a few cacti from the ceiling at different heights. Alternatively, use a floor-to-ceiling plant stand with platforms at various heights to show off their cascading stems. Otherwise, a location on a high shelf works well, too.

You'll often see small white, yellow, pink or red flowers along the stems, followed by berries that resemble baubles. These add a decorative touch, especially when they produce a striking colour contrast.

All the dirt on mistletoe cacti

Light
Mistletoe cacti grow best in bright, indirect light or filtered light. A few hours of direct sun in the morning is ideal, but the surroundings should be bright for the remainder of the day. Avoid lower light levels because these will cause the stems to become thin.

Potting mix
Use a moist, well-drained potting mix, such as two parts premium potting mix blended with one part perlite and one part orchid bark.

Fertiliser
Dilute a liquid fertiliser to half strength, and apply monthly during spring and summer.

Water
Allow the top 2.5-5 centimetres (1-2 inches) of potting mix to dry before watering.

Humidity
Mistletoe cacti are adaptable to the standard level of humidity found in most homes. They will enjoy a little more humidity if you can manage it, but it's not necessary. To maintain a stable environment, it's best to avoid placing the plants near draughts or air-conditioning vents.

Choice species of mistletoe cacti

Mouse tail cactus
(*Rhipsalis baccifera* subsp. *horrida*)

The name *horrida* suggests a rough texture, but this jungle cactus is not at all prickly. Each slender, cylindrical stem is covered in soft, white bristles and resembles a mouse tail, hence the plant's common name. The trailing stems can be up to 30 centimetres in length and offer a great textural contrast with smooth-stemmed species.

Jungle cactus
(*Rhipsalis campos-portoana*)

Long, slender, multi-branched, spaghetti-like stems take on a wild appearance as they fill the pot. The stems initially grow upright before developing their beautiful pendulous form.

Coral cactus
(*Rhipsalis cereuscula*)

This cute species features segmented, knobbly, multi-branched stems that are reminiscent of seaweed. Small, white or yellow, tubular flowers emerge from the stem joins, adding to its charm.

Common problems of mistletoe cacti

Shrivelled stems

Symptom
Stems are shrivelled and limp.

Cause
Underwatering or overwatering.

Solution
Water when the top 2.5–5 centimetres (1–2 inches) of potting mix is dry. While the plant can tolerate periods without water, it's best not to go too long between waterings. The shrivelled stems won't recover, so cut them off with a sharp pair of secateurs.

However, keep in mind that excess water can lead to issues with root rot, which in turn causes stems to shrivel and die. If the plant has been overwatered for an extended period, then remove it from the pot and check the roots. Cut off any soft, mushy roots, and prune dead stems before repotting into a fresh, well-drained potting mix.

Red stems and growth

Symptom
Stems have transformed from bright green to burgundy red tones.

Cause
Heat/sun stress. *Rhipsalis* species are jungle cacti and therefore grow best in bright, indirect light (although a few hours of direct sun in the morning is fine). Too much sunlight can cause the stems to turn burgundy red. Some people like the look of this!

Solution
Move the plant to a spot with bright, indirect light.

White, cottony fluff on stems

Symptom
White, fluffy clusters on stems, often alongside a sticky residue on affected plant parts.

Cause
Mealybugs (sap-sucking insects). The sticky residue is honeydew, a by-product of mealybugs.

Solution
Spray the plant with an insecticidal soap or horticultural oil (such as neem oil or white oil). Try it on a test patch, and check for any negative reactions (such as browning stems or dieback) over a few days before applying it more widely.

Growing tips

Propagate your mistletoe cacti
You'll love how easy it is to propagate mistletoe cacti. For species with thin and stringy stems (cladodes), gather five or six stems and cut them off near the base of the plant (almost level with the potting mix). Cut each stem into 10-centimetre (4-inch) lengths, and insert the base of the cuttings into a pot filled with regular potting mix – you can fill a small pot with 10–15 cuttings. For species with thick, flattened and segmented stems, snip off small segments and insert the base into a pot filled with regular potting mix.

Position the pot in a warm, brightly lit spot, and water only after roots have formed. The plants can be potted into their preferred potting mix once they're established.

Satin vine

Scindapsus pictus

Care
Low maintenance

Pet friendly
No

Light
Bright, indirect light

If you're a fan of the devil's ivy (*Epipremnum aureum*) but searching for something with more flair, then you'll love the satin vine. Often called satin pothos, even within the plant industry, this is incorrect - 'pothos' actually refers to plants in the *Epipremnum* genus, not *Scindapsus*.

There are several cultivars of the satin vine. Their leaves come in varying shades of green, but they all look like they've been brushed with silver. The species name *pictus* is quite fitting because it means 'painted' - this perfectly describes the artistic appearance of the plant's variegation.

People assume that the satin vine has diva-like tendencies, but you'll be happy to know that - like the devil's ivy - it's a relatively low-maintenance plant. In its native environment across Southeast Asia, the satin vine grows as an epiphyte, climbing up trees. Indoors, if it's not provided with support (such as a coir or moss pole), its vines will trail beautifully over the sides of the pot. However, with the right support, it will eagerly climb, mimicking its natural growth habit. Take care when growing it near walls in your home because it has been known to use its aerial roots to attach to and shimmy up interior walls.

Display the satin vine on a shelf or suspend it from the ceiling, so the vines can drape down gracefully. If it has a support structure, then sit it on a table or plant stand where you can fully appreciate its beauty.

All the dirt on the satin vine

Light
The satin vine thrives in bright, indirect light. It's tolerant of lower light, but it will lose its silvery variegation.

Potting mix
Use a premium potting mix blended with some perlite to assist with drainage, such as five parts premium potting mix to one part perlite. If you have an aroid potting mix on hand, then this will work well, too.

Fertiliser
Liquid feed regularly during the warmer months, or apply a controlled-release fertiliser at the beginning of spring, reapplying as directed.

Water
Water when the top 2.5–5 centimetres (1–2 inches) of potting mix is dry.

Humidity
The satin vine is happy with the standard level of humidity found in most homes. However, it will appreciate a little more humidity if you can manage it. For ways to boost indoor humidity, see page 26. Avoid placing it near open windows, heaters or air-conditioning vents.

Choice cultivars of the satin vine

Scindapsus pictus
'Argyraeus'

Sweet, heart-shaped leaves have delicate silver specks scattered across the deep green surface. The leaves are smaller and the variegation is more subtle than in other cultivars, but it still makes for an elegant specimen to display in your home.

Scindapsus pictus
'Exotica'

This is my favourite cultivar! The silver patterning covers most of the leaf, creating a shimmering effect that really stands out. It looks particularly stunning when grown up a coir or moss pole, allowing you to fully appreciate the glittery foliage in all its glory.

Common problems of the satin vine

Leafless stems

Symptom
Sections of the vine have no leaves.

Cause
Insufficient light. After an extended period of inadequate light, the leaves may drop and the vine may be left bare.

Solution
While new shoots may eventually form on these bare vines, it's more effective to cut back the vine to the bushiest part. This encourages new growth. Additionally, reposition the plant to ensure that it has better access to bright, indirect light.

Growing tips

Propagate your satin vine
If your satin vine is looking a little sparse at the top, then you can easily make it lush again by propagating a few cuttings and replanting them.

Grab a sharp pair of secateurs, then follow these step-by-step instructions:

1. Take cuttings that are at least 10–15 centimetres (4–6 inches) long, trimming just below a node (the bump where leaves or aerial roots emerge).
2. Remove the leaves from the lower third of the cuttings.
3. Place the cuttings in a jar of water, a pot filled with propagating mix (a blend of one part general potting mix and one part perlite or washed river sand), or a container of moistened sphagnum moss.
4. Cover the cuttings with a plastic bag or cloche to help maintain a warm, humid environment, but be sure to remove it periodically for airflow.

If you're propagating in water, then wait until the roots reach about 10 centimetres (4 inches) in length before transferring the cuttings to a pot. If you're using propagating mix or sphagnum moss, then keep the medium consistently moist to encourage the roots to develop. This takes four to six weeks.

Peace lily

Spathiphyllum wallisii

Care
Low maintenance

Pet friendly
No

Light
Bright, indirect light

Part of the Araceae family, the peace lily is a favourite among indoor plant enthusiasts. It's celebrated for its easy-care nature, attractive glossy leaves, and distinctive white flowers. Because it's so adaptable, it's a popular choice for shopping centres, offices and homes, and it makes an ideal gift for beginner plant parents.

The flower of the peace lily is actually a spathe - a unique structure that consists of a modified leaf surrounding a cluster of tiny flowers called the spadix. While the spathe is typically white in the peace lily, it comes in various colours among other members of the Araceae family.

You'll find the traditional green-leaved peace lily in most nurseries and garden centres, but the variegated forms can be harder to find. They're worth the hunt, however, especially if you want something a little more special.

The peace lily grows into a large clump, giving the plant a full, bushy appearance. It may get too big for its pot; if this happens, then repot it into a larger container or trough. Alternatively, divide the clump every few years and pot up the divisions.

Although it's rare to hear of someone killing a peace lily, many people still encounter issues with it. Understanding its natural habitat can help to address these problems. The peace lily is native to humid forest floors in tropical Central and South America, where it thrives in dappled light and consistent humidity. While you don't need to give it a greenhouse environment, there are ways to ensure that it looks its best.

All the dirt on the peace lily

Light
The peace lily thrives in bright, indirect light. It can tolerate lower light levels, but it will grow more slowly and won't flower.

Potting mix
Use a premium potting mix.

Fertiliser
Liquid feed regularly during the warmer months, or apply a controlled-release fertiliser at the beginning of spring, reapplying as directed.

Water
Water when the top 2.5–5 centimetres (1–2 inches) of potting mix is dry. Ensure that the water runs through the drainage holes at the bottom of the pot. The leaves will droop quite dramatically if the potting mix becomes too dry - avoid reaching this point because it puts the plant under unnecessary stress.

Humidity
The peace lily is generally happy with the standard level of humidity found in most homes. However, if it's positioned near windows, in draughty areas or close to climate-control devices (such as fans and heaters), the humidity will be lower than it prefers. Browning at the leaf tips typically indicates low humidity. For ways to boost indoor humidity, see page 26.

Choice cultivars of the peace lily

Spathiphyllum
'Sensation'

Often referred to as the giant peace lily, this beauty is known for its large leaves and impressive spathes. It's a true statement plant that makes an ideal floor specimen ... but elevate it on a short plant stand for even more impact.

Variegated peace lilies

Spathiphyllum 'Picasso' (pictured) features broad, white brushstrokes painted across its leaves, while *Spathiphyllum* 'Domino' displays a more subtle stippled effect, as if it has been touched by a delicate hand.

Growing tips

Obtain more peace lilies
The best way to get more peace lilies is to divide your plant! As the plant grows, it naturally forms clumps of new shoots; these clumps can be separated to create new plants. Dividing is best done in spring or summer when the plant is actively growing, giving it the best chance to establish quickly.

To divide your plant, remove it from the pot. Tickle or brush away the potting mix to loosen the roots. Smaller plants or clumps may naturally separate from the mother plant. If they don't, then identify the clumps and ensure that each one has healthy stems, leaves and roots. Use your hands to gently pry the clumps apart. A sharp knife or pair of secateurs may help.

Replant each clump into its own pot filled with a well-drained potting mix, ensuring that the base of the plant is at the same depth as before. Water in well with a diluted seaweed solution, which helps to promote root growth and reduce transplant shock. Place the pots in a warm spot with bright, indirect light.

Common problems of the peace lily

Browning of leaves

Symptom
Brown leaf tips.

Cause
This typically indicates low humidity. It may be the result of draughts or exposure to hot or cool air, which can dry out the air around the plant and lead to water loss from the leaves faster than it can be replenished.

Solution
Position the plant away from open windows or doors to avoid exposure to draughts. Also, keep it away from heating or cooling vents. To maintain consistent moisture, consider placing a shallow tray of water near the plant to increase humidity.

Drooping leaves

Symptom
Leaves have wilted significantly, appearing limp and droopy.

Cause
Underwatering, overwatering or hydrophobic potting mix.

Solution
If the plant is underwatered, then the potting mix will feel completely dry. Give the plant a good soak, ensuring that the water runs through the drainage holes at the bottom of the pot. The plant should recover over the next couple of days (if it doesn't, then this may be an indication that the potting mix has become hydrophobic - see below for the solution). Continue with a more regular watering routine to prevent future issues.

If the plant is overwatered, then the potting mix will feel evenly wet or soggy. Allow the potting mix to nearly dry before watering again, and check if you need to move the plant to a brighter spot or if the pot has sufficient drainage holes. If roots are obstructing the drainage holes, then the plant needs to be repotted into a larger container. If your pot has a saucer, then avoid letting the plant sit in water for any length of time because this can lead to root rot. If the plant is severely overwatered, then it may be best to remove the plant from its pot, prune away any dead, dying or mushy roots, and repot into fresh potting mix.

Over time, potting mixes can become hydrophobic (water repellent), so despite your watering efforts, the water isn't being absorbed into the potting mix. You can rehydrate the potting mix by submerging the entire pot in a bucket of water for 30 minutes, using a brick or similar heavy item to keep it under the surface. Alternatively, use a wetting agent, which is available at most nurseries, to help rewet the mix. The plant should recover over the next few days.

MARTELL
VS
TOKI

Giant bird of paradise

Strelitzia nicolai

Care
Low maintenance

Pet friendly
No

Light
Bright, indirect light

The giant bird of paradise is an impressive specimen. Its large, banana-like leaves impart a bold, tropical look to any space. Indoors, it can reach a height of 2–3 metres (7–10 feet), making it ideal for creating vertical interest. Use it as a stand-alone feature, or cluster it with two other plants - such as *Philodendron* 'Congo' and baby rubber plant (*Peperomia obtusifolia*) - in a trio of pots of varying sizes. A large pot with the giant bird of paradise paired with a medium and a small pot makes for a dynamic display.

Despite its dramatic appearance, the giant bird of paradise is a relatively low-maintenance plant. Native to the subtropical coast of southern Africa, it thrives in warm, humid environments, making it well suited to indoor culture. As it matures, you may notice the leaves begin to exhibit a ripped or torn appearance. This is a natural adaptation that allows the large leaves to withstand strong winds and heavy rainfall in the plant's native habitat.

Because of the size of the leaves, they can easily accumulate dust that may dull their vibrant look. A quick wipe with a damp microfibre cloth will restore their shine; for an extra touch of glamour, consider polishing them with a horticultural oil. This not only enhances their appearance but also helps to treat any sap-sucking insects that are hiding on the foliage - a win-win situation!

All the dirt on the giant bird of paradise

Light
The giant bird of paradise thrives in bright, filtered light. A few hours of direct sun in the morning is ideal, but it needs bright, indirect light for the remainder of the day to maintain its lush growth and vibrant foliage.

Potting mix
Use a premium potting mix.

Fertiliser
Apply a controlled-release fertiliser at the beginning of spring, reapplying as directed. Alternatively, liquid feed regularly during spring and summer.

Water
Water when the top 2.5–5 centimetres (1–2 inches) of potting mix is dry. The plant is somewhat tolerant of longer periods between waterings, but it's still important to monitor the potting mix moisture regularly, especially as the seasons change.

Humidity
The giant bird of paradise is adaptable to the standard level of humidity found in most homes.

Common problems of the giant bird of paradise

White, cottony fluff on leaves and stems

Symptom
White, fluffy clusters on leaves, stems and joints. Affected plant surfaces may have a sticky residue.

Cause
Mealybugs (sap-sucking insects). The sticky residue is honeydew, a by-product of mealybugs.

Solution
Spray affected leaves and plant parts with an insecticidal soap or horticultural oil, ensuring that the solution makes thorough contact with the pests for effective control. Wipe away dead bugs with a cloth. For severe infestations, repeat applications may be necessary.

Silvery or bronzed foliage

Symptom
Leaves have a silvery or bronzed look.

Cause
Spider mites (sap-sucking arachnids).

Solution
Treat with an insecticidal soap or suitable miticide. Check the label for instructions, and use only as directed.

Lumps and bumps on stems

Symptom
Brown, black or coloured bumps on leaves and stems. They can be easily scratched off with your fingernail or a blunt knife. The affected plant parts may also be covered in a sticky residue.

Cause
Scale (sap-sucking insects).

Solution
Spray affected leaves and stems with a horticultural oil, such as neem oil or white oil. It works on contact, so you will need to ensure thorough coverage for effective control. Alternatively, you can use a systemic insecticide that targets sap-sucking insects, or carefully dab a cotton bud soaked in rubbing alcohol directly onto the pests.

Growing tips

Constrain your giant bird of paradise
If your giant bird of paradise becomes too big or wild for your liking, then follow a stem to the base of the plant and use a sharp pair of secateurs to remove the stem. Alternatively, if you want to maintain the majesty of the large plant and you have room outdoors, then place the pot in a sheltered spot outside. Avoid planting the giant bird of paradise in the ground because it can grow up to 8 metres (26 feet) tall and develop thick, dense roots that make it difficult to remove later.

Wild

African violet

Streptocarpus ionanthus (syn. *Saintpaulia ionantha*)

Care
Medium maintenance

Pet friendly
Yes

Light
Bright, indirect light

The African violet deserves more love and attention. While it's not big or showy, its small, fleshy, dark green leaves and sweet, delicate blooms in shades of pink, violet, blue and white brighten up any space. It's the perfect plant for adding a touch of colour indoors with minimal effort.

Once dismissed as an old-fashioned plant, the African violet is making a stylish comeback. Modern cultivars boast intricate ruffled edges, mottled foliage and multi-petal arrangements. With such variety and aesthetic appeal, the African violet is captivating indoor gardeners again.

Due to its compact size, it makes an excellent desk companion. Several plants can be grouped together to create a charming floral display.

I've also seen African violets potted up in glass vessels that feature an inner pot sitting inside an outer pot. Essentially, the larger outside pot acts as a reservoir, while the smaller pot, filled with potting mix, has a wicking ribbon that draws moisture up as needed. This set-up not only adds a modern, stylish touch to your decor but also makes caring for the plants quite easy. The self-watering system helps to maintain a consistent moisture level, reducing the risk of overwatering or underwatering. Plus, when watering from above, the leaves can become easily marked, so using this self-watering method helps to keep the foliage free from unsightly spots. This is especially important for the African violet, as its beautiful blooms and velvety leaves are best showcased without any blemishes.

All the dirt on the African violet

Light
The African violet grows best in bright, indirect light, such as on a windowsill behind a sheer curtain or tilted blinds. Be sure to keep it away from glass or reflective surfaces, as these can transmit heat or cold, which may stress the plant. If there is not enough light, the plant will not flower. Rotate the plant regularly to maintain symmetrical growth.

Potting mix
Use a potting mix created especially for African violets. You can make your own by blending two parts coco peat, one part premium potting mix and one part perlite.

Fertiliser
Feed regularly with a liquid fertiliser specially formulated for African violets. Dilute to half or quarter strength, and apply every time you water.

Water
Water when the potting mix is nearly dry, being careful to avoid getting it on the leaves, as this can cause unsightly brown marks to appear. To prevent this, gently lift the leaves and use a narrow-spouted watering-can to deliver water directly to the base of the plant. Use room temperature or slightly tepid water; cold water can shock and stress the roots.

Humidity
The African violet thrives in a slightly humid environment, ideally around 60 per cent humidity. For ways to boost indoor humidity, see page 26. Keep the plant well away from draughts, heaters and air-conditioning vents, as it doesn't tolerate cold air or dry conditions well. Maintaining an environment that is stable and warm will help to keep the plant happy and blooming.

Common problems of the African violet

Rotting leaves

Symptom
The crown of foliage is mushy, and may appear black or brown.

Cause
Crown rot, caused by overwatering, poorly draining potting mix and/or inadequate pot drainage.

Solution
Unfortunately, if your African violet has succumbed to crown rot, then there is little that can be done. It's best to discard the plant, or try to take cuttings of any unaffected leaves.

To prevent this issue in the future, only water when the potting mix is nearly dry. If the pot is sitting on a saucer or in a cache pot (cover pot), then ensure that the excess water drains away.

Additionally, ensure that the pot always has sufficient drainage, and use a specially formulated African violet potting mix or a moist, well-drained potting mix. Maintain good air circulation around the plant while avoiding exposure to draughts.

Browning petal edges

Symptom
Flowers have brown edges. They may die prematurely, become soft and mushy, or dry out to a paper-like texture.

Cause
Likely to be thrips (sap-sucking insects), but it may also be issues with low humidity.

Solution
Thrips can cause petal edges to brown as they feed on the plant's sap, often hiding on the back of flowers or behind the stamens. They are visible to the naked eye but can be difficult to see, so use a magnifying glass to confirm their presence. Affected flowers may die prematurely or fail to reach their full size, or the buds may never open. To treat, remove the affected flowers and buds, and dispose of them in the bin. Spray the plant with an insecticidal soap or pyrethrum to control the thrips and prevent further damage.

Low humidity can cause flower edges and leaves to brown, and prevent buds from opening. Increase the humidity by sitting the plant on a saucer filled with pebbles and water, or place the plant in a terrarium or cloche, but don't seal completely to allow for air circulation.

Growing tips

Wick this way

A great tip I learned from African violet enthusiasts is to use a wicking system for watering. This technique involves utilising a synthetic cord to draw moisture from a water reservoir below the plant. The cord is inserted through the drainage hole in the pot, with one end in the potting mix and the other end submerged in the water below. This method ensures that the potting mix remains evenly moist without becoming waterlogged, reducing the risk of root rot and water splash on the leaves. It's a great way to water, especially if you're away from home for a week or more.

TARA WIGLEY
SAMI TAMIMI
500
OTTOLENGHI
SMITH & DAUGHTERS
OTK
VEG
CHOCOLATE
COOKERY NOTEBOOKS Claire Joyes

Arrowhead plant

Syngonium podophyllum

Care
Low maintenance

Pet friendly
No

Light
Bright, indirect light

This indoor plant grows quickly and is low maintenance, with minimal problems. What's not to like? It also comes in a stunning variety of patterned forms, adding brightness and interest to your home.

Syngonium species are natural climbers, using their aerial roots to scale trees or structures in the wild. When grown indoors, they appreciate a moss pole or trellis for support. Without one, the aerial roots will spill over the side of the pot in an untamed, trailing manner, which is totally fine if you like a little chaos!

Young plants are perfect for desks, shelves and side tables. As they mature, consider relocating them to larger spaces where they can thrive without dominating the area, such as elevated on a plant stand or grouped with other plants on the floor. Cut stems root well and grow in water, giving you another display option - especially if you want to keep a compact form on your desk or shelf.

Like some popular indoor plants, the arrowhead plant can be a weed - its vigorous habit allows it to spread quickly. This is great for indoor settings but not so much in the garden, so be sure to keep it contained in a pot. Also, when cut, the leaves and stems exude a milky white sap that can irritate the skin and eyes, so take care when propagating or handling the plant.

All the dirt on the arrowhead plant

Light
The arrowhead plant thrives in bright, indirect light, and it will cope with medium light. It can tolerate lower light, but the growth may be thin and stretched out (leggy), and any pattern or variegation on the leaves may fade.

Potting mix
Blend three parts premium potting mix with one part perlite to assist with drainage.

Fertiliser
Liquid feed regularly during the warmer months, or apply a controlled-release fertiliser at the beginning of spring, reapplying as directed.

Water
Water when the top 2.5–5 centimetres (1–2 inches) of potting mix is dry. Ensure that the water runs through the drainage holes at the bottom of the pot.

Humidity
The arrowhead plant is quite adaptable and doesn't mind the standard level of humidity found in most homes. However, if you can provide higher humidity, then it will truly thrive and reward you with more vibrant growth. For ways to boost indoor humidity, see page 26.

Choice cultivars of the arrowhead plant

Syngonium podophyllum
'Fantasy'

A timeless beauty, it has classic dark green leaves beautifully variegated with white. However, it does have a tendency to send out fully green leaves – this is a sign that the plant may be trying to revert to its all-green form. To help maintain its variegation, simply prune it back to a variegated leaf.

Syngonium podophyllum
'Mojito'

This cultivar brings a playful vibe to any indoor plant collection! Its marbled foliage, featuring dark and light green splashes, makes for a striking display.

Syngonium podophyllum
'Pink Splash'

With its dark green leaves splashed, speckled or blotched with pink, this is one of my favourite cultivars. It's such an eye-catching specimen!

Common problems of the arrowhead plant

White, cottony fluff on leaves and stems

Symptom
White, fluffy clusters on leaves and stems, with foliage that feels sticky to the touch.

Cause
Mealybugs (sap-sucking insects). The sticky residue is honeydew, a by-product of mealybugs.

Solution
Spray the plant thoroughly with an insecticidal soap or suitable pesticide. Check the label for instructions, and use only as directed. Repeat treatments may be required. If the infestation is minimal, then carefully dab a cotton bud soaked in rubbing alcohol directly onto the pests.

Growing tips

Promote upward growth
It's not necessary to train your arrowhead plant to grow up a support (such as a moss pole), but this will keep the plant tidy and also give you a better view of its leaves. You can buy a support or make your own (see page 193). Some are simple stakes that you insert into the pot, while others are wire cylinders that need to be weighed down by potting mix.

Once the support is secure, select a vine, gently press it against the support structure, and fasten it using garden ties, twine or soft fabric (such as hosiery). Make sure that a node (a bump on the stem where leaves or aerial roots emerge) is in contact with the support. Over time, aerial roots will naturally cling to the support; you can then remove the ties.

Spiderworts

Tradescantia spp.

Care
Low maintenance

Pet friendly
No

Light
Bright, indirect light

With their brightly coloured foliage and, for some species, waxy texture, spiderworts (*Tradescantia* spp.) are hardy and attractive indoor plants. Known for their trailing habit, these plants thrive in various conditions and add charm as they spill over pots. *Tradescantia zebrina* - a purple-leaved variety with metallic silver or grey-green markings - is the most common form, but there are others with cream, pink or green variegations.

Commonly referred to as spiderworts due to their rapid growth and spreading habit, they are best kept indoors - even discarded cuttings in the garden or compost heap can easily take root and spread. Make sure that you bag cut stems before throwing them in the bin, or submerge them in water for a few weeks or until they begin to rot, ensuring that they can't resprout. This prevents any unwanted plant growth in your garden or elsewhere. On the plus side, this trait also makes spiderworts simple to propagate, so you can easily expand your collection or share plants with friends.

Their trailing habit makes spiderworts ideal for displays where they can cascade elegantly over the edges of pots, hanging baskets or shelves. You can also mix them with other plants for a dynamic arrangement; this creates a lush, layered look that adds depth and interest. I've seen this done beautifully in front of a frosted window in a bathroom - spiderworts inject so much life into a space!

All the dirt on spiderworts

Light
Spiderworts thrive in bright, indirect light. Some species can tolerate direct sun, but too much can scorch their leaves. They can tolerate lower light but may become leggy and lose their colour as a result.

Potting mix
Blend five parts premium potting mix with one part perlite to assist with drainage.

Fertiliser
Liquid feed with a diluted indoor plant fertiliser when the plant is actively growing during spring and summer.

Water
Water when the top 2.5–5 centimetres (1–2 inches) of potting mix is nearly dry. While spiderworts can generally withstand long periods without watering, it's important not to let them dry out completely.

Humidity
Spiderworts aren't picky about humidity and thrive in the standard level of humidity found in most homes.

Choice species and cultivars of spiderworts

Tradescantia albiflora **'Albovittata'**

Subtle yet striking, this cultivar features soft green leaves with delicate white stripes. The leaves are thicker and more succulent-like than those of *Tradescantia fluminensis* 'Variegata' (see below).

Tradescantia **'Blushing Bride'**

An interesting hybrid, it has soft blush pink to white variegations that are more prominent during the cooler months. Once the weather warms, the pink becomes less pronounced and leaves appear more green.

Tradescantia fluminensis **'Tricolour'**

You'll love the eye-catching combination of white, pink and green in the variegated leaves, accented by pink stems. The pink in the leaves becomes more pronounced with light exposure, so be sure to place it in a brightly lit spot.

Tradescantia fluminensis **'Variegata'**

If pink doesn't suit your style, then this is a great option. It features only creamy white and green variegations, creating a fresh and elegant look without the added colour.

Common problems of spiderworts

Long, leggy, stretched-out growth

Symptom
The space between the nodes is elongated, and the plant no longer looks compact and bushy. Sections of the stems may be leafless.

Cause
Insufficient light.

Solution
Move the plant to a spot where it can receive more light, ensuring that it's protected from direct sun. Prune back growth to areas where it's most bushy; this will encourage new growth and help to restore a fuller appearance.

Growing tips

Propagate broken stems
Have you accidentally broken off part of your plant? Don't worry - turn it into a new plant! Spiderworts are some of the easiest plants to propagate because they root readily in potting mix or water.

Remove the lower leaves from the broken stem, and place the stem into a glass of clean water, ensuring that at least one node (the bump where the leaf emerges) is submerged. Alternatively, insert the broken stem into a pot filled with propagating mix (a blend of one part general potting mix and one part perlite or washed river sand), and water regularly to keep the potting mix moist. You can also take a 10-15-centimetre (4-6-inch) cutting from the end of a healthy stem, trimming below a node, and place the cutting in water or propagating mix.

Joan Blond.

ZZ plant

Zamioculcas zamiifolia

Care
Low maintenance

Pet friendly
No

Light
Bright, indirect light

Whenever someone asks, 'What should I buy for a plant newbie?' or 'What can I grow in a room with low light?', my go-to answer is the ZZ plant.

The ZZ plant features small, glossy, dark green leaves on elegant, upright or slightly arched stems. These fleshy stems are designed to store water, making the plant resilient to dry periods and capable of surviving occasional underwatering. If you examine the roots, then you'll find small, potato-like structures called rhizomes, which also store water (and nutrients). This adaptation also allows the ZZ plant to thrive even with infrequent watering. However, this doesn't mean you should neglect your plant entirely!

Many people refer to this plant as unkillable – and I must admit that I've said this myself. While it's indeed more tolerant of neglect than most houseplants, it's important to note that it can still be killed if you completely ignore it or only provide sporadic care. Doing so will lead to a slow decline, and watching a plant suffer is never enjoyable. So, it's best to give it some consistent attention to keep it happy.

In its native dry grasslands of eastern Africa, the ZZ plant can die back completely during periods of extended drought. This happens because the plant conserves energy and resources by retreating to its rhizomes. When rainfall returns, the ZZ plant uses the stored energy in the rhizomes to grow back and re-establish itself.

All the dirt on the ZZ plant

Light
The ZZ plant is adaptable to a range of light levels. It grows best in bright, indirect light, but it will also tolerate lower light conditions. While it won't thrive, it will survive and continue to add greenery to your space.

Potting mix
Use a well-drained potting mix made for cacti and succulents, or blend two parts premium potting mix with two parts sand and one part perlite.

Fertiliser
Apply a controlled-release fertiliser at the beginning of spring, reapplying as directed.

Water
Water when the top 2.5–5 centimetres (1–2 inches) of potting mix is dry. The ZZ plant can tolerate long periods without water, often going one or two months between waterings, although it may need more frequent watering if it's placed in a warm, brightly lit spot or regularly exposed to draughts.

Humidity
The ZZ plant is quite forgiving when it comes to humidity, adapting well to a variety of levels.

Choice cultivars of the ZZ plant

***Zamioculcas zamiifolia* 'Heemsprix'**

Also known as Jungle Warrior™, this is a striking plant! The new leaves are bright green, and they age to dark purple-black. At first I wasn't a fan because the black reminded me of sooty mould, but it's definitely grown on me. It's tough like its green counterpart.

***Zamioculcas zamiifolia* 'Zenzi'**

A dwarf form of the classic ZZ plant, it only grows to about 30 centimetres (12 inches) tall and wide. It's cute and an ideal desk companion.

Growing tips

Propagate your ZZ plant
If you have a mature ZZ plant that's outgrowing its pot, then you can divide it into smaller plants by carefully removing it from the pot and then separating it into sections. Make sure that each section has a healthy root ball and stems so it can thrive independently.

If your plant isn't ready for division, or you prefer a simpler approach to propagation, then stem or leaf cuttings are great alternatives. Snip a healthy stem, and keep it in a jar of water until roots develop. Or, cut off a leaf at the base where it attached to the stem, and insert the cut end into a container filled with perlite, keeping it consistently moist to encourage root growth. With a little patience, you'll soon have new ZZ plants to enjoy or share!

Common problems of the ZZ plant

Yellowing leaves, poor growth

Symptom
Leaves and stems yellow and die back, and there is little to no new growth.

Cause
Overwatering, insufficient light or the plant becoming root-bound.

Solution
If the plant is overwatered, then the potting mix will be consistently soggy or wet. Excess moisture in the potting mix because of overwatering or poor drainage leads to root rot, which impacts the plant's ability to take in water and nutrients. Leaves and stems may yellow, becoming soft and limp. Remove the plant from the pot, and assess the roots. Tease away the potting mix and cut off any rotten, mushy roots, then prune back the yellowing stems to ground level. Repot into fresh potting mix, and only water when the mix is nearly dry.

If you have placed the ZZ plant in a room where there is little to no light, then this can lead to yellowing leaves and poor growth. The ZZ plant can tolerate periods of low light, but extended periods of little to no light can cause the stems to weaken and collapse. Move the plant to a spot with more light; if this isn't possible, then consider grow lights. Prune weakened stems to encourage new growth.

Over time, the roots of the ZZ plant can completely fill the pot, taking up all of the available air pockets and depriving the plant of water, air and nutrients. This can ultimately starve the plant and stunt its growth. You may see roots poking through the drainage holes, or if you give the plastic pot a squeeze, then there won't be much give. If your plant is in a terracotta or ceramic pot that can't be squeezed, then you may need to gently remove the plant from its pot to assess the roots. To fix a root-bound plant, remove the plant from its pot, gently tease out the roots, and repot it into a larger container with fresh potting mix.

Acknowledgements

Writing this book was far from a solo effort, and I'm deeply grateful to everyone who generously offered their time, knowledge and support along the way.

First and foremost, this book wouldn't have been possible without my publisher, Melissa Kayser. I had never considered writing a book, but your guidance and belief in this project helped me to see its potential and bring it to life.

I'm immensely grateful to the Murdoch Books publishing team - Melissa Kayser, Virginia Birch and Megan Pigott - for your expertise, patience and guidance throughout this process; to my editor, Dannielle Viera, whose skill in refining my words and offering thoughtful, constructive feedback made this manuscript the best it could be; and to the designers and illustrators, Bonnie Eichelberger and Amelia Leuzzi, thank you for your creativity and artistic vision.

Capturing all of these photos of plants in various pots and homes was no easy feat, but the photographer, Chris Chen, and creative director, Megan Pigott, rose to the challenge. I'll always remember our days together - obsessing over whether to include a figurine, adjusting the angle of a pot, and our shared excitement over the beautiful locations.

These stunning shots were only made possible thanks to those who generously welcomed us into their homes: Gordon Giles, Ted and Yvette Pigott, Naomi Van Groll, Katrina Chew, Keren Moran and Noa Peer, and Graham and Sandra Ross, whose photogenic spaces provided the perfect backdrops. I'm also grateful to Megs for sharing your own lovely home and to Chris for the use of your studio.

A heartfelt thanks to Gordon Giles and Keith Wallace of Keith Wallace Nursery for their warm hospitality, welcoming us into their nursery (and Gordon into his home!) and treating us to morning tea and even lunch.

Several of the plants featured in this book were generously loaned by Gowan Stewart (@queenplants_) and David Fripp, two remarkable collectors and growers whose kindness is truly appreciated.

To my horticultural friends - Eric Bharucha, Matt Gerakios, Louise Liu, Steph Robson and Steve Falcioni - your camaraderie, advice and thoughtful feedback have been invaluable throughout this journey. I can't forget Roger Fox, my former mentor and dear friend, who took me under his wing at *Better Homes and Gardens* magazine and nurtured my writing skills and furthered my love of gardening.

On a personal note, I am deeply grateful to my parents, my inspirations and pillars, whose strength and sacrifice have guided me throughout life and led me down this garden path.

To my husband, Alfonso, I love you. Your unwavering support, enthusiasm and can-do attitude have meant everything to me. And to our gorgeous daughter, Ayla, who was with me every step of the way. From the long days and late nights spent writing the manuscript to the photoshoots and the early days of reviewing the draft once you were earthside - you were there for it all. Mama loves you.

Finally, thank you for purchasing this book. I hope it has helped you flourish and thrive as a plant parent.

Index

D

E

F

G

R

S

T

U

W

Y

Z

Published in 2025 by Murdoch Books, an imprint of Allen & Unwin

Murdoch Books Australia
Cammeraygal Country
83 Alexander Street
Crows Nest NSW 2065
Phone: +61 (0)2 8425 0100
murdochbooks.com.au
info@murdochbooks.com.au

Murdoch Books UK
Ormond House
26-27 Boswell Street
London WC1N 3JZ
Phone: +44 (0) 20 8785 5995
murdochbooks.co.uk
info@murdochbooks.co.uk

For corporate orders and custom publishing, contact our business development team at salesenquiries@murdochbooks.com.au

Publisher: Melissa Kayser
Editorial manager: Virginia Birch
Design manager: Megan Pigott
Designer: Double Slice Studio | Bonnie Eichelberger & Amelia Leuzzi
Editor: Dannielle Viera
Production manager: Natalie Crouch

Murdoch Books acknowledges the Traditional Owners of the Country on which we live and work. We pay our respects to all Aboriginal and Torres Strait Islander Elders, past and present.

EU Authorised Representative: Easy Access System Europe, Mustamäe tee 50, 10621 Tallinn, Estonia, gpsr.requests@easproject.com

ISBN 978 1 76150 071 8

A catalogue record for this book is available from the National Library of Australia

A catalogue record for this book is available from the British Library

Colour reproduction by Megan Ellis
Printed in China by C&C Offset Printing Co., Ltd.

10 9 8 7 6 5 4 3 2 1